The Case for Civility

The Case for Civility

And Why Our Future
Depends on It

Os Guinness

HarperOne
An Imprint of HarperCollins*Publishers*

HarperOne

HarperCollins books may be purchased for educational, business, or
sales promotional use. For information please write: Special Markets
Department, HarperCollins Publishers, 10 East 53rd Street, New York,
NY 10022.

HarperCollins Web site: http://www.harpercollins.com

HarperCollins®, ▲®, and HarperOne™ are trademarks of
HarperCollins Publishers.

FIRST EDITION

Library of Congress Cataloging-in-Publication Data:

Guinness, Os.
The case for civility : and why our future depends on it / Os
Guinness.—1st ed.
    p. cm.
ISBN: 978-0-06-135343-7
ISBN-10: 0-06-135343-4
  1. Courtesy–United States. 2. Conduct of life. I. Title.
BJ1533.C9G85 2008
177'.1—dc22   2007043399

08 09 10 11 12 RRD(H) 10 9 8 7 6 5 4 3 2 1

DOM,
And to Jenny and CJ,
my two beloved Americans.

So, let us not be blind to our differences—but let us also direct our attention to our common interests and to means by which those differences can be resolved. And if we cannot end now our differences, at least we can help make the world safe for diversity. For, in the final analysis, our most basic common link is that we all inhabit this planet. We all breathe the same air. We all cherish our children's future. And we are all mortal.

—PRESIDENT JOHN F. KENNEDY,
Commencement Address, American University,
June 1963

Contents

Chapter One

A World Safe for Diversity

It would be a safe but sad bet that someone, somewhere in the world, is killing someone else at this very moment in the name of religion or ideology.

Currently, the world's newspapers give us each day our daily read of the Sunni Muslims ferociously slaughtering Shia Muslims in Baghdad, and of Shia Muslims ferociously slaughtering Sunni Muslims in revenge. Elsewhere it might be Muslims and Hindus killing each other in Kashmir, or Buddhists and Hindus in Sri Lanka, or Muslims and animists in Sudan. Earlier it would have been Protestants and Catholics in Ulster, and Muslims, Orthodox, and Catholics in the Balkans. These are just some of the infamous examples of the carnage, and the devil is usually in the detail of the images and words. As one radical Muslim's placard declared with a stunning lack of self-consciousness: "Behead those who say Islam is a violent religion."

But before anyone drifts off into the well-rehearsed litany of blaming it all on religion, we should remember that modern "terror" began in France in 1789 in the name of secular Reason, killing several million in its wars and committing a near-genocide in the Vendée on its first outing. Nearer our own time, close to a hundred million people were slaughtered in the twentieth century by secularist regimes, led by secularist intellectuals, in the name of secularist ideologies—far more than the deaths from all the religious persecutions and repressions in Western history combined.

In the world's most murderous century, about one hundred million human beings were killed in war, another hundred million under political repression, and yet another hundred million in ethnic and sectarian violence.[1]

Unquestionably, religion can be divisive, violent, and evil. But, also unquestionably, secularism can be oppressive, murderous, and evil, too. Leaving aside Hitler, who was anti-Christian but not an atheist, Lenin, Stalin, Mao Tse-tung, Pol Pot, the Young Turks, and the Spanish Republicans were all secularist, though cut from the same cloth as Osama bin Laden and Abu Mus'ab al-Zarqawi. When priests and nuns were slaughtered by the thousands and churches sacked and destroyed in the Spanish Civil War, a Republican wrote: "These burnings were the autos da fé necessary for the progress of civilization."[2]

This is no moment for crowing by either side, or for cheap attacks and mindless finger-pointing by anyone. There is enough blame to go around to sober us all, and the urgent need is for solutions, not scapegoats. As Ambrose Bierce pronounced with bitter accuracy in *The Devil's Dictionary*, "The defining feature of humanity is inhumanity."[3]

But the point at which we must begin to respond is to face up to the core of the dilemma today: How do we live with our deepest differences, especially when those differences are religious and ideological? The place at which we must begin to search for answers is the United States. Not because the problem is worse here than elsewhere—on the contrary—but because America has the best cultural resources, and therefore the greatest responsibility to point the way forward in answering the deepest questions.

This short essay is a proposal for restoring civility in America, as one model for fostering civility around the world and helping to make the world safe for diversity. But civility must truly be restored. It is not to be confused with niceness and mere etiquette or dismissed as squeamishness about differences. It is a tough, robust, substantive concept that is a republican virtue, critical to both democracy and civil society, and a manner of conduct that will be decisive for the future of the American republic.[4]

Let America Be America

"Let America be America." That maxim is not a statement of jingoism or empty bombast when written by a foreigner. Yet if ever there was a time for Americans to live up to the saying and save it from becoming a cliché, let alone a form of rank hypocrisy, it is now. The alternative is to let things slip, and accelerate the moment when the need will be to save America from herself.

As history's first new nation and the current lead society in the modern world, the United States is distinctive for the way it was founded by intention and by ideas. American ideals and institutions do not trail off into the mists of antiquity as do those of many nations. They were born in an unprecedented burst of brilliant thinking and political building, and from the very beginning they engaged constructively with many of the central challenges and characteristic features of the modern world.

Freedom, equal opportunity, the rule of law, mutual responsibility, representative government, the separation of powers, freedom of religion, freedom of speech, freedom of assembly, justice grounded in due process and the presumption of innocence, universal public education—as words, these ideals trip off the tongue lightly; but as principles, they form the bedrock on which the greatness of America has been built.

Earlier, many people around the world were blind to the significance of what George Washington called "the great experiment" and the founders declared "the new order of the ages." Unlike Alexis de Tocqueville, such people did not see the meaning and importance of the rise of democracy in America. And while their traditional ways of life endured, they could afford to ignore it.

That is no longer the case. The global era has thrust almost all the world into the same avalanche of change and choice, so that many formerly traditional countries are now scrambling to come to terms with modern problems for which their traditions and customs have not prepared them.

Witness, for example, the once-homogeneous British and Dutch scrambling to adapt their traditional views of tolerance to a whirlwind of disruptive diversity undreamed of a generation ago; or the hauteur of the French at being forced to renegotiate their strictly secular way of public life under the impact of Muslim immigration while still pressing to keep any reference to Europe's two-thousand-year Christian past out of the preamble to the European Constitution. Both of these are the sort of challenges that the United States has wrestled with from the very beginning; and for anyone willing to learn, the American experience is highly instructive.

Ironically, however, at the very moment when the world is ripe for a new appreciation of the significance of the American experiment, two things block the United States from being the "city upon a hill" so often cited by Americans from John Winthrop to Ronald Reagan. The more obvious but lesser problem is that recent American policies have alienated the world as never before. The less obvious but larger problem is that the United States is not performing so well itself in areas where once its accomplishments were thought to be a proven success.

To put the point plainly, much of the world is not currently inclined to watch or listen as they might, and America is not modeling the American way of life as once she used to.

Nowhere is America's failure to live up to her own promise more striking than over the thorny issues surrounding liberty, diversity, and unity—or the question of how Americans live with their deepest differences. E Pluribus Unum has long been both America's motto and its greatest triumph, but the troubled front lines of America's culture wars show a very different reality. The challenge of living with deep differences is calling into question not only freedom and justice but America's very identity—and this at a time when living with our deepest differences has become one of the world's greatest issues, one that cries out for new and urgent solutions on a wider scale.

This essay is a proposal for reforging civility in American public life—a tough, robust democratic civility wrested from the jaws of the culture wars.

I write as a longtime European admirer of the United States, with the deep conviction that the quest for civility in world affairs has to begin in America; but also with a growing sadness that America's recent leadership has not matched up to her global responsibilities. It is not that the American Way should be the world's way, or that there is a one-size-fits-all solution for world civility, for there are multiple modernities, and each nation must work out a solution that suits its own unique culture and history. It is rather that civility stands a better chance of success in America than in any other major country, because of the resources of American first principles, such as freedom of conscience. It is true, too, that success in the world's leading society would provide a stronger example and be a brighter beacon to the rest of the world.

For who can doubt that living with our deepest differences is one of the world's greatest issues?

Pandaemonium

"Now the crusades have ended." Those words, uttered by General Edmund Allenby when he entered the Holy City of Jerusalem on December 9, 1917, invoked the memory of Richard Coeur de Lion, leader of the Crusading forces of Western Christendom. Like a later American president's "Mission accomplished" in Iraq, Allenby's rash claim was soon to be contradicted but never forgotten. More accurate, though no less inflammatory, was the declaration of the French governor who entered Damascus in 1919 and visited the tomb of the great Kurdish warrior Salah Ad-din Yusuf. Placing his gun on the sarcophagus, he said, "Saladin, we have returned."[5]

If there are ghosts in the Balkans, the ghosts in Palestine and in the wider Near East are older and even more implacable. For three thousand years, believers and infidels of one faith or another—from the Israelites and Philistines, to the Egyptians, Assyrians, and Chaldeans, to the Jews and the Greeks and the Romans, to the Franks and the Turks, to the Saracens and the Mongols, to the Western Allies and the Ottomans, to the Yankees and the Islamists, to the Shias and the Sunnis—have fought across the terrain with clubs and slingshots, swords and scimitars, chain-mail armor and assassins' cloaks, tanks, Humvees, and suicide martyr belts.

Muslims today may fight under the banner of the Prophet, but Arab leader after Arab leader also fights for the honor of picking up the mantle of Saladin, the scourge of the crusaders. The Old Man of the Mountains, leader of the dreaded assassins, stalks the world again in the form of Osama bin Laden; and even the would-be assassin of Pope John Paul II wrote that he had intended to slay "the supreme commander of the Crusades."[6] Sixty years ago, the English writer Hilaire Belloc predicted today's dramatic resurgence of Islam, and also pointedly warned that Muslims would seek revenge for their last great humiliation in Europe—at the siege of Vienna in 1683; to be precise, on September 11, 1683.

And still today, as for countless centuries, the "thrice-Holy City" of Jerusalem is at the storm center of it all, with the modern nation of Israel taking roughly the place of the twelfth-century kingdom of Jerusalem, and certainly being seen as intrusive to many of its surrounding Muslim neighbors, as the crusader kingdom was to the Turks and the Saracens of its time.

No wonder, then, that the official name for Osama bin Laden's al Qaeda ("the base") is "The World Islamic Front for Holy War Against Jews and Crusaders."

History, of course, is only one ingredient in the clash and din of Middle Eastern strife. Add others, such as religious and theological differences, the struggle for power and vital resources such as oil, the potent human passions for identity and justice, the dark currents of vengeance and honor, not to speak of advancing technologies of communications right down to the Internet. And before you know it, you have a witches' brew of ancient hatreds and conflicts, as ready to be brought to the boil today as it was a thousand, two thousand, or three thousand years ago.

Then lift up your eyes and follow the trail of blood around the world, and you see that the problems of the Middle East are only one of the world's chronic flashpoints. The twentieth century climaxed with a gory explosion of ethnic and sectarian violence that offset its equally striking march of freedom after the fall of Soviet tyranny. Bosnia, Kosovo, Rwanda, Congo, Sierra Leone, Sudan, Burma, Chechnya, East Timor, northern Uganda—the litany of massacres was a grim reminder of the crooked timber of our humanity, and together they created a bloody crescendo to Europe's most evil century and the world's most murderous.

What accounted for this rash of savagery, war crimes, ethnic cleansings, and genocides, and this after the horrendous early- and mid-century evils to which a shocked world had vowed "Never again"? Words such as *primitive, primordial, elemental,* and *atavistic* were used frequently to warn of the special and unspeakable horror of what was about to be described. And a long list of ideologies and -isms was brandished wildly in the desperate attempt to clutch for satisfying answers. Such acts were said to be the bastard offspring of nationalism, ethnocentrism, fascism, chauvinism, racism, fundamentalism, militarism, terrorism, xenophobia, failed and failing states, or just simply human hatred.

Beyond any doubt, the ferocity of the sectarian violence beggared words and left even hardened observers reeling from the sight of such a dark harvest of hatred and cruelty. What does it say of us as human beings that those who did these things are the same species as we are, and that under certain circumstances we might have done these same things? The dreadful series of mini-holocausts was a humanitarian nightmare and a cauldron of ancient hatreds and animosities. To use Senator Daniel Patrick Moynihan's word, it could be described only as "Pandaemonium"—John Milton's name for the high capital of Satan and his devils.

More sobering still, as Darfur and Burma continue to demonstrate with mute agony, we have not yet seen the end of it. With swelling human numbers on the planet, persisting religious and ethnic divisions, mounting inequalities between rich and poor, shrinking natural resources such as water, spreading risks and hazards in the global era, and the tsunami-like effect of instant, total information through technologies such as the Internet, such conflicts will only worsen, and their debris will wash up on all our shores.

Far from Francis Fukuyama's blithe "end of history" and the neoconservatives' rose-tinted vision of the universal triumph of a single, sustainable model of freedom, democracy, and free markets, the New World Order looks to be growing ever more disordered—with zones of anarchy and semianarchy, failed and failing states, terrorism, unconventional wars, illicit trade and human trafficking, and the growing danger of conflicts over the scarcity of natural resources.

Such unstable conditions are ever vulnerable to asymmetric violence, and certain brute facts confront those of us privileged to be citizens of the world's strongest and most prosperous nations: that economic and military dominance do not translate into security, that complete safety is a myth, and that fear rather than confident trust is for many people a rational response to the world in our time.

In 1963, President Kennedy summed up what has come to be one of the supreme challenges for humankind in the global era: "If we cannot end now our differences, at least we can help make the world safe for diversity."[7]

Uncomfortable but Unavoidable

In the face of this titanic task, I present in this essay a serious proposal for civility in American public life, accompanied by a constructive proposal for how to achieve this goal. The global situation calls for responses on many levels, some of which at the moment present situations that are frankly intractable. But I believe something can and should be done in America, and I see five considerations that form the challenge that confronts Americans.

First, and most important, Americans must face the fact that the challenge of living with our deepest—that is, our religiously grounded—differences is one of the world's great issues today. Allow me to underscore the point.

How do we live with our deepest differences as human beings?

How do we live together as humans when such differences are religious and ideological differences, and when these religious and ideological differences are absolute, ultimate, and irreducible, so that it becomes evident that what divides us is deeper than what unites us?

How do we live together when we acknowledge that these differences are not just a matter of private worldviews but of "comprehensive doctrines" and *entire ways of life,* each with its own claims and requirements that cannot help but impinge on the ways of life of others?

How do we live together when we realize that the deepest of these differences are not just between different countries and civilizations but within the same society?

And how do we live with such deep differences on a planet where travel and the media are shrinking our world and on which we are all thrown together so that it is said that everyone is now everywhere, and on which technologies such as the Internet mean that we can often be overheard by everyone else even when we are not speaking to everyone else?

Do our deep differences now spell disaster? Are our improved communications an inevitable cause of intensified conflicts? And will the very faiths by which we make sense of ourselves and our lives prove to be the fault lines that will endanger human society and the planet itself? Or, expressed more directly for the United States, how do Americans ensure that the motto E Pluribus Unum remains an accomplishment rather than words no longer lived by?

Such questions clamor for constructive answers. Yet to this point there has been more decrying the darkness than offering any light. And of the responses put forward, most have been ill considered and inadequate. A call for civility is far more than a well-meaning admonition to cool it and lower our voices.

Second, all members of the world's educated classes must face the fact that the perspective that has dominated Western thinking about religion for more than a century—namely, the secularization theory—is seriously flawed and damaging in its influence. To be carefully distinguished from the philosophy of secularism (according to which there is no such thing as God, gods, or a supernatural), the theory of secularization purports to explain the fate and future of religion in the modern world.

Claiming Europe's experience as their pattern for the world, secularization theorists have argued that modernization necessarily entails the decline and disappearance of religion—so that the more modern a nation becomes, the less religious it also becomes. But if Europe was therefore the vanguard, the United States was recognized as the one possible exception. Because of its unique historical circumstances, it bucked the trend and was both the most modern country in the world and the most religious of modern countries.

This view of secularization, trumpeted by many as "progressive, universal, and inevitable," has been decisively called into question. We are living, however, between the lightning and the thunder, and public discussion, including much educated opinion, has yet to catch up with the better understanding. The last thirty years have witnessed a much-needed revision of secularization theory. Today, following the Iranian revolution of 1979 and an explosion of varied evidence from around the world, it is widely recognized that secularization theory is empirically wrong, and that all too often it has been philosophically biased as well. The theory simply does not do justice to the realities of human experience in real life in today's world.

For one thing, in the words of the eminent sociologist Peter L. Berger, the overwhelming evidence is that "religion is as furiously alive as ever."[8] For another, the United States is no longer held to be the exception, though two important exceptions have taken its place. One is geographical—the secularity of Europe, although closer study shows that Europe is

not as secular as it was once thought to be. The other exception is social—the secularity of the educated classes, a highly
significant fact because of the dominance of the educated
classes in key sectors of modern society where their tone-
deafness about religion has wider consequences for others:
above all, in the universities and colleges, in the press and
media, and in the discussion of international relations.

This crucial revision of the secularization theory is note-
worthy, but more is at stake than academic accuracy. As we
shall see, there are deeper practical issues that need to be
considered. On the one hand, there is the question of justice
and freedom for those whom secularization theory has victimized. On the other, there is the recognition of the irony
that as the theory of secularization has weakened, the philosophy of secularism has grown stronger, or at least louder—
the result being a secularist fundamentalism that matches the
rise of religious fundamentalism and creates one of the two
poles of today's extremism in religion and public life.

The net effect of this intolerant secularism must be assessed
with the same clear-eyed realism that we use to assess the
menacing rise of fundamentalism and religious extremism.
From the murderous coercions of communism, to the forced
silences of French secularism, to the brazen intolerance of the
new atheists, Europe and many of the educated classes in
other parts of the world have developed a way of thinking
that has excluded religion from public life more decisively
than at any other time in human history. That this unprecedented attitude and its policies may be just as damaging to
freedom as religious extremism must be considered.

*Third, the global era is raising a brand-new issue for our
time—the emergence of a global public square.* Originally
rooted in the Greek *agora* and the Roman forum where

citizens assembled to discuss public affairs, the term "public square" no longer refers to a physical or literal place on the order of London's Trafalgar Square, Washington's Lafayette Square, or Paris's Place de la Concorde. It is simply a metaphor for all the forums in which citizens can come together to deliberate, debate, and decide the implications of their common life. As such, it covers both the formal expressions of the public square, such as the British Parliament, the American Congress, and the French Assembly, and the informal expressions of the public square, such as the op-ed pages of our newspapers, the radio talk shows, coffee-shop discussions, and the burgeoning Web logs.

From the Greeks onward, notions of the public square have been central to Western ways of thinking. The highest ideal in Athens was not to be a "tribesperson," someone who was simply a member of a group—or an "idiot," the word for a purely private person—but a "citizen." In the famous words of Pericles, "this is a peculiarity of ours: we do not say that a man who takes no interest in politics is a man who minds his own business; we say that he has no business here at all."[9]

Recent developments in the West represent what Richard Sennett has described as "the fall of public man."[10] But many of the old public-square issues are coming into focus again as modern technologies of communication—supremely, the Internet—are fostering the emergence of a truly global public square, evident at both the elite and the popular levels.

At the elite level, globalization means that those once apart are now brought together and are seizing every chance to discuss common global affairs—epitomized by the World Economic Forum in Davos. Similarly, at the popular level, globalization means that those once apart now bump into each other through the effect of travel and the media, creating new forms of culture shock—demonstrated in the recent well-coordinated Muslim rage in response to Salman Rushdie's novels and knighthood, to certain Danish cartoons, and to Pope Benedict's recent speech at Regensburg University.

The simple fact of the global era is that we can be over-heard by the world even when we are not aware that we are talking to the world. How, then, do we live with our deepest differences when more people, with more diverse perspectives and more possible reasons to differ and disagree, can hear us than ever before?

Fourth, as I said, Americans must face the embarrassing fact that just when the world is ready to notice the significance of the American way of being modern, many aspects of the American way are under severe stress and are hardly capable of being a model for anyone. In particular, the culture wars are threatening to call into question many of the foundational assumptions of what it is to be American.

To be sure, it is as dangerous to exaggerate the culture wars as it is to minimize them.[11] At the core of these wars is a battle between two sets of elites, with their corresponding battalions of activists, organizations, and supporters. And on most issues, the great majority of Americans find themselves between the two sides, somewhat ambivalent and often confused. But when all the issues have been clarified and matters of style separated from matters of substance, it becomes clear that the issues dividing the traditionalists and the progressives are important and will be decisive for the future of the republic. They are, after all, disagreements about the very nature and destiny of human beings, so they cannot be swept under the rug.

In short, the issues at the heart of the culture wars will be decisive for the American future, and they will have to be settled—but not in the present, destructive manner.

The current style of discourse in the American culture wars forms a black hole into which the fundamental principles and striking successes of the republic are being drawn and destroyed. For more than thirty years I have been a sustained and outspoken critic of the culture-warring style of both extremes, and I wish to propose a solution decisively different from both: a vision of a cosmopolitan and civil public square in which such important differences may be deliberated, debated, and decided in a way that protects and promotes both liberty and unity.

It is time for Americans to reforge a civil public square, to wrest back the culture wars from the domineering pundits and activists who have become the warlords of American public life—and then to debate such important issues as the uniqueness of humanity, the character of life and death, the importance of truth, the relationship between virtue and freedom, and what the historian Gertrude Himmelfarb described as "the collapse of ethical principles and habits, the loss of respect for authorities and institutions, the breakdown of the family, the decline of civility, the vulgarization of high culture and the degradation of popular culture."[12]

To remain passive before the bullying of the cultural warriors on issues such as these is both foolish and dangerous, for the outcome of these issues will determine the future of the United States at a moment when to miss the way is to court national decline.

Put differently, Americans again have to choose whether they still value the *res publica* ("the public thing"), the covenanted partnership whose goal is a common vision for the common good, a goal that lifts their republic above a democracy. If Americans do choose the republic, they must attend to civility, which is a form of republican "second nature," a cultivated "habit of the heart" that lifts citizens above the Hobbesian "state of nature" and the war of all against all. If they do not, America will become a bare democracy, counting heads, brokering interests, and declaring winners and losers in a long-running grand game of nickels and noses.

So the question is: Are "we the people" still dedicated to abiding by a covenant of constitutional relationships that requires duties as well as recognizing rights, that gives weight to truth, justice, and restraint as well as to power, and that sees civility as a necessary and vital companion to freedom and justice for all?

Law and the rule of law are fundamental to freedom, just as politics is to republican democracy. But when it comes to settling cultural issues, law is a cudgel rather than a scalpel. It is not the right instrument for solving all the issues raised in the culture wars. Worse, the habitual resort to unrestrained law is producing a litigious spirit that is spreading across American civility like a cancer. Worst of all, the constant resort to rights-based, ultimate judicial solutions rather than a twin reliance on political debate and a robust popular civility is devastating American common life.

Americans at large must recognize that culture warring does not do justice to the fundamental Jewish notion of covenant and the classical notion of a republic—notions that underlie America.

Culture warring seriously distorts the way Americans understand their own history.

It insults the brilliance of the framers' provisions for negotiating difference.

It offers neither a solution nor an alternative to the dilemmas posed by the ethnic and sectarian conflicts around the world.

It bedevils the possibility of resolving many contentious but vital issues today.

Worst of all, it spells disaster for America, because it poisons the cultural soil that nourishes freedom and undermines the framers' provisions for sustaining freedom that are at the heart of the republic.

Fifth, the developments and conflicts over religion and public life of the past generation are coming to a head in a way that could produce a watershed moment for the United States. From the rise of the Religious Right in the mid-1970s to the role of the Religious Right in the election of George W. Bush in 2004, the tide has flowed powerfully in the direction of conservative religious influence. The tide is now turning. The tie-in between the Religious Right and the Republican Party, and in particular between the Religious Right and the person and policies of George W. Bush, has provoked a mounting backlash that has made the liaison a severe liability for both.

The antireligious backlash can be seen at the popular level—for example, Rosie O'Donnell's recent claims on an ABC talk show that conservative Christians are even more dangerous than Muslim terrorists, and the comparison, on NBC's *Studio 60 on the Sunset Strip,* of Christians to Ku Klux Klansmen.[13] But the backlash is far more lethal in educated and liberal circles, where it can be seen in the explosion of attacks on the Religious Right, either in the name of opposing views of religion and public life or in the name of a vehement, reenergized, and openly intolerant secularism—for example, such books as Sam Harris's *End of Faith* and *Letter to a Christian Nation*, Richard Dawkins's *The God Delusion*, and Christopher Hitchens's *God Is Not Great.*

This backlash portends far more than a pendulum swing in political fortunes. Following the crisis of cultural authority that grew out of the 1960s, it may indicate a seismic shift in the foundations of the American republic that will change America forever.

We shall explore all these five considerations in greater depth as we proceed, but it would be a mistake to dismiss them as purely theoretical, or to see them as only another swing of the pendulum. They may sound abstract, especially when put alongside such dramatic topics as international terrorism, HIV-AIDS, nuclear proliferation, global warming, dirty bombs, and the specter of bird flu or mad cow disease. Yet far more people have died, and far more will die, through bad or faulty ways of living with our human differences than as a result of all these other problems combined. How we live with our deepest differences is a question that lies at the heart of American freedom, and soon it may be a matter of survival for the planet. Americans have both high ideals and a wealth of experience to share with the wider world.

A Truce of God

What am I proposing in this essay? I am setting out a vision of civility in the American public square that, if realized, could be the key to resolving the culture wars, could be a stunning tribute to the brilliance of the "great experiment" devised by the American founders, and also could stand as an encouragement and as a model for public civility to be considered in other parts of the world.

Why the American public square? For countless reasons, the prospects for civility in the global public square in the short term are bleak. Immanuel Kant's vision of "perpetual peace" and the Enlightenment dream of a single, universal civilization are utopian and unrealizable. But the first, best chance for civility in the world is the United States. On the one hand, America has been wrestling with the dilemmas longer, with better foundational resources, and with a generally better outcome than in any other nation. On the other hand, in spite of recent problems such as the culture wars, America has still not developed the levels of extremism that bedevil solutions elsewhere.

Why a proposal by an outsider, someone who is both a visitor to America and a Christian? By the very nature of the problem, no one stands outside the issues and speaks with complete detachment, objectivity, and neutrality. Certainly I do not. None of us speaks from nowhere; that would be impossible. None of us speaks from everywhere; that would be incoherent. All of us speak from somewhere—which is our freedom and responsibility as well as our fate.

In the present contentious circumstances, candor can be clarifying. I speak and write as I live, as a follower of Jesus Christ and a visitor to the United States. In the present circumstances, both perspectives are a burden and an advantage. The burden starts with the present American prickliness about foreign views of the United States and the baggage of the Christian past, for rarely has America's standing in the world been so low. And clearly, Christians have at times talked of the Prince of Peace but flagrantly betrayed him with their dark record of state-sponsored coercion and violence from Constantine to the eighteenth century. The latter burden comes right down to the present, for certain Christians form the bulk of one of the two great extremes in the American culture wars and are stirring up against themselves some of the most vehement antireligious animosity in the modern world. There will be issues on which I shall disagree as emphatically with many of my own fellow Christians as I do with some of their strongest opponents.

But there is an advantage, too, in writing as a Christian and a foreigner. The Christian faith is not only the world's most numerous faith but the world's first truly global faith, so its present stand for civility today, along with its struggle for justice and freedom, is of world historic significance. What is more, the teaching and example of Jesus, as opposed to that of certain of his followers and certain other religious leaders, is unambiguously on the side of justice, peace, and civility. Also, the distinguished Christian contribution to America's proud record on religious liberty—along with the contribution of certain Enlightenment thinkers—means that a Christian call for civility grows naturally from the heart of the Christian faith and can be backed by a wealth of principle as well as pragmatic urgency.

Why a truce—or, as I am tempted to say, a "truce of God"? A truce, of course, is a cessation or suspension of hostilities with the agreement of the two opposing sides. In the same vein, the "truce of God" was the Christian term for the medieval church's attempt to limit and suppress the violence of feuds, family quarrels, and private wars that were tearing Europe apart in the tenth and eleventh centuries. The details of the original medieval truce of God need not concern us. I am using the term here as a metaphor to capture two ideas that were central to the original concept:

First, there are people for whom conflict should be a contradiction of all they stand for (in the medieval case, conflict between fellow believers; in modern America, between fellow citizens).

Second, summary private responses to disagreements (in the medieval case, characteristically violent; in modern America,

*through the myriad ways of culture warring) are to be replaced
by orderly processes of settling disputes.*

Needless to say, a truce succeeds not when it is proposed but
rather when it is accepted and maintained, and can therefore
lead to genuine peace, in the Jewish sense of profound communal well-being based on justice and security. I therefore write
as a Christian, but I am not primarily writing *to* Christians.
My question to readers is whether enough people of other
faiths, and enough leaders in key spheres of American life, will
consider and respond to this proposal to create the will to
change the present disastrous course and chart a better way.

Having stated the overall challenge, let me sketch an outline of the journey we will take. First, in chapter two, we will
explore how three main settlements have dominated the
Western response to the challenges of religion and public
life: the French, growing out of the Revolution of 1789; the
English, shaped by the Glorious Revolution of 1688; and the
American, formed by the First Amendment in 1791. Of these
three settlements, the American is the most original, the most
conducive to freedom and justice for all in pluralistic conditions, and the one that James Madison justifiably called "the
true remedy."[14]

Second, in chapter three, we will look at the fact that, for
all the three great settlements' long shadow over two to three
centuries, there are signs that each of these settlements is in
trouble. The reasons are different in each case, but each in its
way has so far proved incapable of accommodating certain
modern developments. In the case of the United States, the
outcome of the breakdown is the culture wars, of which the
bitter and divisive conflicts over religion are the holy war
front. Such are the levels of the tensions that a new settlement, adequate for our times, is required.

Third, in chapters four and five, we will examine the different models for understanding the public square, and in particular we will identify the extremes that provide the boundary markers in the debate. On the global stage, the two extremes that define the terrain are a *strict coercive secularism,* once represented by Soviet communism and now by a shrewder Chinese communism and a softer but strict French secularism, and a *radical fundamentalism,* represented mainly by Islamism but with more moderate parallels in other religions, too.

Expressed differently, two options are now being put forward in terms of how we are to relate to others in the global public square, and both have a tendency to swing toward the extremes. On one side are the *progressive universalists,* those who believe that their way is the one way, the way for everyone, even at the cost of coercion—a position that leads inevitably toward *conflict.* And on the other side are the *multicultural relativists,* those who believe that all cultures are different and that there are no universal values, and that therefore no one has the right to judge another culture or its values, let alone intervene in the affairs of another culture and impose his or her values on another culture. More tolerant-sounding at first, this option is also an extreme because it leads to *complacency.* If we are never able to judge or intervene in the affairs of others, we will inevitably turn a blind eye to evil, injustice, and oppression.

Narrowing the field to the American public square, we can see that the extremes have long been defined as two opposing answers to how religion and public life should be related to one another. On one side are the advocates of a *sacred public square,* the "re-imposers" who would give a privileged place to one religion at the expense of others; and on the other side are the advocates of a *naked public square,* the "removers" who would antiseptically cleanse the public square of all religion.

Fourth, in chapter six, we shall look at what is meant by a *cosmopolitan and civil public square,* clarifying the misunderstandings and confusions that surround this concept and detailing what it would take to reestablish a civil public square in the midst of the culture wars. Crucially, we will see the difference between the common *dialogue approach* to civility, which I shall argue is attractive in the short run but finally ineffective, and the *covenant approach,* which alone holds the key to a worthwhile truce and a tough-minded civility.

Finally, in chapter seven, we shall look in broad terms at what needs to be done to restore civility, and in particular how we must start with ourselves before looking to leaders to change the quality of public life at the highest levels.

The Williamsburg Charter: A Proposal

Beyond the proposal outlined in this essay, I cannot go. I am not an American citizen, and the responsibility for taking up the initiative must lie with Americans. I would certainly hope that, from ordinary citizens, to religious leaders, to educational leaders, to political leaders, to national leaders, and to presidents and presidential candidates, Americans at all levels will pick up this issue, and will do so soon, before it is too late. But let me recount two experiences that give this issue a personal urgency for me.

The first occurred in China in the wintry early months of 1949, when I was seven and living with my parents in Nanking, the ancient Ming dynasty city that General Chiang Kaishek had made his capital twenty years earlier. Remorselessly, the People's Liberation Army of Mao Tse-tung had swept down from the north under Lin Bao and was menacing the Yangtze heartland and the Nationalist capital. Along with other Westerners, I had met both Chiang and his American-educated wife, Soong Mei-ling, so it came with a touch of personal shock when my father told me on a bitterly cold day at the end of January that the general and his entourage had flown out of the city that morning and left it to the mercy of the Red army.

We knew of the unspeakable brutalities of the earlier rape of Nanking under the Japanese, and we had heard reports of the staggering death toll in the Nationalist armies, as well as rumors of horrific outbursts of cannibalism and other atrocities in the cities ravaged by the Communists. We were soon to experience the reign of terror—the public trials in which children informed against their own parents and parents against their own children, and then the public executions. But all the swirl of rumors and fears suddenly took on a terrifying face for me when the city changed overnight after the Communists marched in on April 23, 1949—Saint George's Day and William Shakespeare's birthday.

Instantly, friends I had played and partied with a few days earlier passed me by in the street, looking right through me, not daring to acknowledge my presence. To know a Westerner, or a "blue-eyed foreign devil" as the taunt of the crowds put it, was more than their lives were worth. Many of my friends' parents and teachers and the leaders in Nanking's burgeoning churches simply disappeared for good—the first wave of what became the millions of Chinese arrested, imprisoned, tortured, and killed at the orders of the Great Leader who, in the name of his grandiose utopianism, slaughtered so many of his own people and became the greatest mass murderer in history.

For the next two years I lived with my parents under house arrest, with angry mobs often swirling outside and numerous threats and insults hurled at us. Eventually, my father and mother were able to entrust me to an American friend, later a Princeton professor, who was passing through Nanking and who accompanied me to Hong Kong and safety. Three years later, my parents themselves were released. Those were intense, frightening, sobering days, and they have left an indelible imprint on my view of the world and of the precariousness of life. Certainly they deepened my later appreciation for the bedrock preciousness of such rights as habeas corpus, freedom of conscience, freedom of speech, and freedom of assembly—which leads to the second experience behind my concerns today.

In the summer of 1986, I was a visiting fellow at The Brookings Institution in Washington, D.C., completing some research on the genius of the religious-liberty clauses of the First Amendment. Through fortuitous circumstances, a summary I had written in a tribute to the success of the First Amendment fell into the hands of Senator Ted Stevens, who had just been appointed to the Commission on the Bicentennial of the U.S. Constitution. He called and invited me to lunch with Chief Justice Warren Burger, his close friend and the chairman of the bicentennial commission.

During the course of the lunch, Chief Justice Burger said that, although there were countless bicentennial projects celebrating free speech and free assembly, there were no major projects celebrating the religious-liberty clauses. What would I suggest? After a fascinating discussion on the brilliance of the religious-liberty clauses, he invited me to address the members of the bicentennial commission in Annapolis and to consider what might be a suitable commemoration of the first sixteen words of the First Amendment.

What I proposed was the Williamsburg Charter, an official bicentennial celebration of the First Amendment religious-liberty clauses that had two objectives: first and more straightforwardly, to celebrate the unique genius of the religious-liberty clauses and their decisive influence on American history; and second and more constructively, to set out a vision of a restored civil public square that would do full justice to the genius of the religious-liberty clauses today and invite the free participation of citizens of all faiths and none in the continuing American experiment. As such, the Williamsburg Charter represents a key part of what is required for the broader renewal of American freedom today. (The Williamsburg Charter was named after Virginia's colonial capital, which witnessed a historic milestone in the history of human rights with the passing of Virginia's Declaration of Rights in May 1776.)

The charter was drafted over the course of the next two years by a representative group of writers in open consultation with leaders from all the faith communities as well as with scholars and experts from such fields as history and law. The drafters included Nat Hentoff, the veteran First Amendment defender and *Village Voice* reporter; the late Dean Kelley of the National Council of Churches; then pastor and now Father Richard John Neuhaus; George Weigel, later an eminent papal biographer; and me.

The Williamsburg Charter was signed on June 25, 1988, in front of the Hall of the House of Burgesses in Williamsburg, in a historic ceremony on the two-hundredth anniversary of Virginia's Bill of Rights. Signers included former presidents Gerald Ford and Jimmy Carter, Chief Justice William Rehnquist, and wide variety of American leaders from all spheres of society.

The Williamsburg Charter is the leading statement of American religious liberty in the twentieth century. It would be fair to say that it was a substantive success though a political failure: strong opposition from the Religious Right blocked the participation of President Reagan, whose backing was crucial to the practical rollout of the Charter in spheres such as public education. It is probably true, too, that some of the signers signed the charter for reasons of bicentennial patriotism rather than the seriousness of pledging their lives, their fortunes, and their sacred honor—and so did not take it with the seriousness that we hoped for, or that the issue deserved.

Also, after living in the United States for some time now, I would have to say with sorrow that America is suffering a severe inflation of words and ideas, and therefore of commitments. Hollowed out by the specious lies, half-truths, and nonsequiturs of ceaseless advertising and by other factors such as the ubiquity of ghostwriting, American verbal commitments do not mean what they once did. In a world of "words, words, words," someone's saying that their word is their bond is not so much a commitment as a rhetorical flourish or a piece of pious nostalgia.

The vision represented by the Williamsburg Charter is needed more today than when it was first proposed. The charter itself is included at the end of this essay as a model and a proposal. The vision and the substance of a civil and cosmopolitan public square are there, but the potential has not yet been translated into political reality. It awaits American citizens and an American leader willing to step forward and pick up the challenge of restoring civility to American public life. Nothing less than the sustaining of America's own freedom is at stake, as well as America's privilege of standing again as a model for the world.

Chapter Two

The True Remedy

A few days before his death in July 1898, the German chancellor Otto von Bismarck is supposed to have shared with a friend his premonition about the coming century. "What would be the decisive factor in the next century?" he mused. "The fact that Americans speak English." With hindsight, his prediction looks obvious, though it was far from obvious at the time. In Bismarck's day the British Empire was the largest, strongest power on earth, but within twenty years it had declined and begun to fade, and the vacuum was filled not by Germany or any victor of a European conflict of powers, but by the United States. The result was what Henry Luce hailed in 1941 as "the American century."

A hundred years after Bismarck, no single factor appears decisive for our times. Instead, the complex global world of the twenty-first century confronts a series of grand questions, the answers to which will decisively shape the next fifty to one hundred years. Three are especially urgent.

First, will Islam modernize peacefully, forswearing its tendency toward militancy, pacifying its violent extremists, reversing its low view of women, acknowledging the right of religious liberty for all, including those Muslims who convert to other faiths, and accommodating to the fact of social diversity? Or will its continuing violence, its insistence on coercing faith, and its adamant refusal to allow faith to be privatized be the catalysts that force the modern world to reconfigure its structures and policies, either for better or for worse?

Second, which faith will replace Marxism as the dominant ideology in China as the Middle Kingdom reemerges on the world stage as a superpower and responds to the opportunities and challenges of forces such as capitalism, democracy, and massive social change?

And third, will Western civilization sever or recover its Jewish and Christian roots—either severing them according to the pattern of state-favored European secularism or recovering them according to the better angels of the American experiment?

As a moment's thought would show, these three momentous questions are neither accidental nor isolated. They are each linked with the other two as different responses to modernity, they are all strongly reinforced by the processes of globalization, and they each have a clear religious dimension as well as a strategic and geopolitical dimension.

Indeed, when we explore these questions, and when we bring them together with issues raised by globalization for the future of the planet, it becomes obvious that—for better or worse—the place of religion in world affairs in the coming century will be salient and unavoidable. The French writer and statesman André Malraux may have come closer than anyone else to the central issue of our time: "The twenty-first century will be religious, or it will not *be*."[1]

A Joker in the Pack

The salience of religion in our times is a massive stumbling block to much educated opinion in Europe, the United States, and the Western world at large—to what was once called the republic of letters, and which Peter Berger calls "the international faculty club."[2] For one of the cardinal assumptions of intellectual orthodoxy since the Enlightenment, expressed canonically in the secularization theory, is that modernization means secularization, which in turn means that, like Lewis Carroll's Cheshire cat, religion will slowly disappear from sight as the world modernizes, leaving behind only a vacant grin.

This presumption translates practically into three attitudes that are widely prevalent in educated circles in the West: that religion in the modern world is irrational, archaic, retrograde, and on the way out; that what remains of religion is the leading source of evil and conflict today; and that a central task of politics is to curb the illiberal power of religion, above all in the public square. In short, the idea that religion is a wild card in human affairs is admissible, but the idea that it could play a central and constructive role is absurd.

For any thoughtful student of world affairs who understands the role of religion in American and Western history, or in international affairs today, this view is preposterous. It flies squarely in the face of facts, and it rests on premises that are unexamined as well as secularist. What is out of step, Berger notes, is not the religiosity of the world but the secularity of the observers. ("The difficult-to-understand phenomenon is not Iranian Mullahs but American university professors.”[3])

We may leave it to events to disabuse the prejudice, and to future ages to explain it. One does not have to agree with Thomas Aquinas that unbelief is contrary to human nature, with Edmund Burke that man is by constitution a religious animal, or with Berger that religion is a perennial feature of humanity to see that, at the very least, the prejudice is the product of what Max Weber called the tone deafness of certain elites: they do not hear or appreciate the music by which most people have, do, and always will orchestrate their lives. Sam Harris’s vision of the “end of faith” is as much wishful thinking as Francis Fukuyama’s “end of history.”

Whatever the source of the prejudice, the tone deafness has to be taken seriously because it affects public life and the freedom of many citizens whom those who are prejudiced simply do not take into account because their faiths are reckoned to be on the way out like an ebbing tide. The historian William Lee Miller captures the comic side of the “unmusicality” in the remark of an attorney: “What is the matter with these people? Why do they persist? Millions of those people out there believe what nobody believes anymore.”[4]

The tone deafness also has to be taken seriously because of its effect on international relations. The war on terror, for example, demonstrates a second dimension of asymmetrical warfare that goes beyond technology and weaponry. Islam is not a monolith, and Islam as a whole is not fighting either the West or the Christian faith. But Osama bin Laden and the Islamists are self-consciously fighting a religious war (“This war is fundamentally religious ... Those who try to cover this crystal-clear fact ... are deceiving the Islamic nation”), and they see themselves confronting a modern world both created and represented by an explicitly religious enemy ("World Christianity, which is allied with Jews and Zionism").[5] So when the West, which has outgrown the Christian label and no longer recognizes the heart of the conflict as religious, insists instead that the roots of the war lie in poverty, lack of education, the results of foreign policy, and the impact of globalization, it is fighting at cross-purposes with its enemy and is prone to misunderstandings and blunders.

The most charitable explanation of this tone deafness is that many educated people do not realize that their social world is one of the two great exceptions to the general religiosity of the wider world—the other exception being geographical rather than social: Europe. Europe is unquestionably different from the United States, because of its different history.[6] But even there, contrary to the belief that modernization means secularization and the disappearance of religion, many European countries are post-Christian but not secular, and the United States stubbornly bucks the trend altogether. *America is both the most modern nation in the world and the most religious of modern nations.*

What is clear is that the notion of secularization as the inevitable decline and disappearance of religion in the modern world is the secularist's fond hope, if not superstition. Religion in America and in most parts of the world is not disappearing and shows no sign of disappearing; and even in those parts of the world where it has declined for the moment, there are indications that the story is not over.

For better or worse, religion is an unavoidable fact of modern life; and if it is not to be for the worse, it will have to be understood and engaged constructively. Liberals would therefore do well to face facts, swallow any personal disappointment, and join a more constructive, civil—and truly liberal—discussion of the issues raised. Those who dismiss the importance of religion in human affairs court ignorance and condemn themselves to folly and failure in their practical policies.

If this point is understood, it underscores two things: Europe, not the United States, is the world's exception for the moment; and the United States, not Europe, is the more reliable bellwether to help us assess the future of religion in world affairs.

It is even arguable that "secular Europe," far from being the world's vanguard of attitudes toward religion, may not even be the model for her own future. For the signs are that European "secularity" is not as secular as it cracked up to be. Part of the secularity, as can be seen in the story of the French Revolution, is a direct reaction to the earlier corruptions of religion, but this secularity may well breed a reaction to itself in turn. Jefferson long ago noted the role of reaction in shaping such faith when he observed that defections from Protestantism were often milder and in the direction of deism, whereas "in Catholic countries they are to Atheism."[7]

More important, the sociologist Grace Davie qualifies the stark view of European secularization with a series of nuances that cast it in a different light. First, what was once thought to be secularization is more accurately a form of believing without belonging, as religious beliefs persist while allegiance to institutional forms of religion declines.[8] Second, what remains is often a form of "vicarious religion," as those who have no religious affiliation still continue to look to established churches to speak on their behalf and sustain the cultural memory of their country at key moments in national life—such as Britain's outpouring of national grief after the death of Princess Diana.[9] Martin Rees, Britain's present

Astronomer Royal and president of the Royal Society, famously acknowledged that he goes to church as an "unbelieving Anglican ... out of loyalty to the tribe."[10]

In sum, even in secular Europe reports of the demise of religion are greatly exaggerated. The poet Matthew Arnold, who heard the tide of faith receding on Dover beach with its long reverberating roar, should have remembered that the same tide that goes out comes back in.

Regardless of Europe's future, what matters here is America's present as the world's leading society. The practical effect of the incomprehension surrounding faith in America has been captured in two witty and perceptive observations by Peter Berger. On the one hand, he remarked, the tone deafness of the elites at home means that United States is "a nation of Indians ruled by Swedes."[11] In other words, the American people are as religious as the people of India, the most religious country in the world, whereas the American elites are as secular as the people of Sweden, the most secular country in the world—a fact that lies at the core of the culture wars today.

On the other hand, Berger has observed more recently, a similar tone deafness abroad means that America is paradoxically viewed in many parts of the world as a nation of "Puritans and pornographers."[12] In other words, there is a striking contradiction between foreign intellectuals' reaction to the powerful religious and moral forces evident in America, unusual because of the unusual strength of religion, and the equal though different popular reaction to the purported decadence of American culture, also unusual because of the unusual strength of American freedom and consumerism.

Indians and Swedes, Puritans and pornographers—the combined effect of all these kinds of incomprehension obscures a clear understanding of America and its significance for the world.

The American Settlement

America's characteristic emphasis on her written Constitution and her equally emphatic contrast with England's unwritten constitution obscures a simple but important fact. For much of America's history, there was an unspoken understanding of how religion and public life should be related, an understanding that amounted to an unwritten constitution that accompanied the written Constitution. In other words, there was an implicit and broadly shared understanding that was a "habit of the heart," an informal settlement, or—in the sense that all covenants are designed to order a way of doing things—the American way of religion and public life.

It goes without saying that this unwritten understanding has broken down in the last fifty years, leaving us with the written Constitution alone and with incessant conflicts over religion and public life. But this informal settlement was not only the broad result of the First Amendment; it was a unique American way that stood in clear contrast to the French and the English settlements that represented the two dominant European patterns of religion and public life at the time. Just as it is now recognized that there were three distinctively different Enlightenments—the French, the British, and the American—so it should be seen that there were three different settlements of religion and public life.

In the case of each settlement, a revolutionary year— 1688 for England, 1789 for France, and 1791 for the United States—became formative for the nation's decisions about religion and public life, and the resulting arrangements have cast a long shadow down the centuries. What is striking, however, is that in the first two cases there is a clear link between yesterday's established religion and today's secularization.

At one extreme, 1789 was decisive in pushing France in a radically secular direction—or, as Jefferson said, toward atheism. A deeply corrupt church and a deeply corrupt state had united in their coercive repression of all dissent, and, like a volcanic explosion, the French Revolution blew them both away together: the Jacobin slogan of "strangling the last king with the guts of the last priest" had the effect of producing Jefferson's full-blown atheists rather than moderate deists like himself.

Expressed more carefully, the Gallican Church, which was traditionally hailed as "the eldest daughter of the Church" and ruled by "the most Christian king" of France, had resisted all internal efforts toward reform, whether Protestant or Jansenist. But the price paid for such recalcitrance was the buildup of a hurricane of pressures from the outside. Suddenly the storm broke in the form of the revolution, and in a few short years France went from her age-old "altar and throne" to the short-lived church and revolution to the final revolutionary religion.

In less than a decade, a highly political religion morphed into a highly religious politics, the first of such sacred causes or totalizing ideologies that were to be the scourge of Europe in the twentieth century. Watching the French Revolution from England, Burke wrote of "Atheism by Establishment," and in France itself in 1792, Mirabeau observed, "the Declaration of the Rights of Man had become a political Gospel and the French Constitution a religion for which people are prepared to die."[13] The Church militant of the Middle Ages had collapsed of its own corruptions, and in its place arose the Reason militant of the Enlightenment, washed in the blood of the guillotine and marching forward under the seemingly invincible banner of Napoleon's battalions.

Church and state were not officially separated in France until February 21, 1795. But the overall explosion that the corrupt, coercive French establishment ignited against itself created a grand fusion of revolution and irreligion and led to a radical secularization of French public life, so that in France to be progressive still mostly means being secular and to be religious still means being viewed as reactionary. This is a key part of the French mentality that lingers to this day and bedevils the resolution of French conflicts over religion in public life, not to speak of the direction of the European Union.

Astonishingly, too, Roman Catholic writers, from the popes down, who decry the militancy of French secularism today rarely acknowledge that this fierce secularism was bred and developed in direct reaction to their own earlier corruptions and has led to similar outbreaks of murderous anticlericalism elsewhere. These include the vicious Mexican repression of Catholics in the 1920s and the brutal Socialist slaughter of seven thousand priests, nuns, and bishops in Spain in 1936.

In 1688 in England, the settlement was different and so also was the result. The move toward secularization was discernible but slower, more moderate and more fitful—all because of a very different establishment. To be sure, the Glorious Revolution kept the Church of England as the established national church, but even the church's critics granted that it was half reformed; and while there was open discrimination against the nonconformists, it was relatively mild. There was no wholesale repression, and there was no English equivalent of the Saint Bartholomew's Day massacre, let alone the slaughter in the Vendée.

As a result, English history has never been characterized by the militant anticlericalism or the wilder extremes of French secularization. Yet the secularization has been steady if slow, and the Church of England today hardly seems more than a beautiful Gothic ornament in English public life, or a nationalized utility for the "hatching, matching, and dispatching" of citizens, rites of passage in the seasons of life. Remembering Davie's important qualifications about "believing without belonging" and "vicarious religion," we should not dismiss this reduced role altogether. But Davie is equally clear that the church has indeed "lost its role as the keystone in the arch of European culture."[14] Though still established, the Church of England is little more influential in England than the long-disestablished Catholic Church in France.

The year 1791 and the passing of the First Amendment put the United States at the other extreme from the start. Religion in America was clearly and decisively disestablished, but it flourished all the more—not so much in spite of disestablishment as *because of it*. Without the insidious embrace of church and state, religion in America was liberated to be a matter of free, voluntary, independent choice, dictated by conscience alone. It was therefore cut free from the deadly entanglements through which European religion had come to be the parent of its own secularization and the digger of its own grave.

In the famous comment of the twenty-five-year-old Alexis de Tocqueville, visiting the United States in 1831 as a Frenchman, a nobleman, and a Roman Catholic in a largely

Protestant country, "On my arrival in the United States, it was the religious atmosphere that first struck me. As I extended my stay, I could observe the political consequences which formed from this novel situation. In France I had seen the spirit of freedom moving in the opposite direction to that of the spirit of freedom. In America, I found them intimately linked together in joint reign over the same land."[15]

The word *reign* was no idle metaphor for Tocqueville. A few pages earlier, he commented even more provocatively, "Religion, which never interferes directly in the government of Americans, should therefore be regarded as the first of their political institutions."[16]

First Liberty

Religion as "the first of the political institutions"? Many today would bristle at such words, fearing that they suggest a turn toward the "Christian America" of the Religious Right. They would therefore like to turn the United States in the opposite direction and toward a radical French-style secularization of public life. So it is important to assess what the earlier and now lost settlement once meant to America, and what its complete dismissal will mean for America's prospects of sustainable freedom in the future.

Only a romantic or a diehard would see America's early record as all sweetness and light. There were terrible violations of religious liberty before the Revolution, such as Boston's entirely lawful arrest, trial, sentencing, and hanging of the Quaker Mary Dyer in 1660. And for all its brilliance, the First Amendment had a major flaw and a serious inconsistency. The flaw was that—contrary to Madison's determined efforts at the Constitutional Convention—the First Amendment limited the federal government's power to restrict religious liberty, but not the power of the states to do so. The inconsistency was that religious liberty was widely understood to apply to Protestants but not to others in the same way. More numerous than others, Protestants were also more equal than others.

Madison considered his proposed article, which limited the power of the states over religion, "the most valuable amendment on the whole list."[17] But it was struck down. If the Convention had followed Madison in 1791, a century and a half of struggles could have been avoided. Thus the subsequent development of the American settlement from 1791 to the end of the World War II includes many violations of religious liberty as the flaw and the inconsistency were worked out.

The worst of the violations were the vicious outbreaks of bigotry expressed in the Know-Nothing movement, with its virulent nativism, anti-Catholicism, and anti-Semitism. The early years of the republic also witnessed the long, arduous task of removing the last vestiges of religious tests and established churches in various states. And then, after the Civil War, when the Fourteenth Amendment applied the First Amendment rights and restrictions to the states, too, it did not make clear how the two halves of the religious-liberty clauses should now be understood at the state level, which has been a bone of legal contention ever since.

Thus Madison's "true remedy" was not in fact implemented consistently, and, like all things human, it has been less than perfect. First, indelible stains on the American record stand for all time as a check on triumphalism and a reminder of the need for humility. Second, unresolved constitutional tensions and inconsistencies remain to this day and are a reminder that law alone can never provide the magic formula to solve the problems. And third, since religious liberty as a natural human right is prior to and independent of all government decisions, including those of the Supreme Court, no genera- tion's interpretation of the First Amendment will ever be the last word on what religious liberty means. The highest court in the land has the last word on the law, but not on interpret- ing religious liberty. Just as twentieth-century decisions had to revisit nineteenth-century decisions, so the same will be true for twenty-first century decisions. Equal religious liberty for all is an ongoing quest, not an achievement that ends the struggle once and for all.

But these reminders also need to be held in perspective. The worst violations of the past were eventually overcome, America's record on religious liberty is infinitely better than that of the other two European settlements, and the construc- tive breakthrough in religious freedom was achieved much earlier than America's eventual success in either slavery (abol- ished long after it was in Europe) or democracy (nearly fifty years after the Revolution, only 5 percent of American adults voted in the presidential election; and women were granted the right to vote only in 1920). In sum, to harp on the viola- tions of religious liberty in America's past, as some secular- ists do, and to forget the even more egregious and recent violations of democracy and racial justice is both churlish and short-sighted. In America, illiberalism in matters of reli- gion was tackled earlier and much more successfully than illiberalism in matters of race and sex.

In sum, the story of the American settlement is one of a broad and increasingly tolerant picture of religion in the young republic. This picture deserves deeper appreciation today, for many of its features were deeply liberal, even if they have to be significantly adjusted in light of contemporary conditions and challenges. Three features of this unwritten settlement characterize the American settlement at its best.

First, the First Amendment's ordering of religion and public life may reasonably be called "the true remedy" because it does justice to the founders' understanding of religious liberty as "the first liberty." Today, religious liberty is often reduced to "liberty for the religious" and treated as a nonissue or a nuisance. At best it is considered a second-class right, inferior to freedom of speech and freedom of assembly. At worst it is treated as a constitutional redundancy, the removable appendix of the Bill of Rights, and the ugly stepsister to the more fashionable civil liberty. Like Victorian children who were to be seen but not heard, religious liberty today is to be private but never public.

It was not always so, and for the sake of freedom it should not be so. As a twenty-two-year-old James Madison wrote to a friend, William Bradford, "The rights of conscience ... is one of the Characteristics of a free people."[18]

Religious liberty, or freedom of conscience, is a precious, fundamental, and inalienable human right—the right to reach, hold, freely exercise, or change one's beliefs, subject solely to the dictates of conscience and independent of all outside, especially governmental, control.

Religious liberty is a right that is grounded in the inviolable dignity of the human person, and in particular in the character of reason and conscience. For people of faith, this right is to be respected as a gift from God and a duty to God: In the words of Jefferson's "Bill for Establishing Religious Freedom," drafted in 1779 and passed in 1786, "Almighty God had created the mind free ... who being Lord of both body and mind, yet chose not to propagate it by coercions on either."[19]

For others, the right of religious liberty is a fundamental consequence of human nature itself and of our capacity as thinking, choosing, conscience-directed beings. And for both, this foundation in human dignity is what makes religious liberty a natural, basic, and indispensable right, independent of the decisions of any group or government. As a human right rather than a favor, religious liberty is a right to be guaranteed by the government, but it is not the government's right to grant.

Religious liberty is for all human beings, not simply liberty for the religious. It is rooted in the characteristic, natural, and inescapable human drive toward meaning and belonging. As fundamental as life itself, this "will to meaning" finds expression in ultimate beliefs, whether theistic or nontheistic, transcendent or naturalistic. Religious liberty is for atheists and secularists, too, and for all human beings who assume and value meaning in their lives.

Religious liberty, as a gift of God and a consequence of human dignity, does not finally depend on the discoveries of science, the favors of the state and its officials, or the vagaries of tyrants and majorities. It is therefore a right that may not be submitted to any vote or encroached upon by the expansion of the bureaucratic state.

Religious liberty is a right that was prior to, and existed quite apart from, the Bill of Rights that protected it. As a free-standing right, it is integrally linked to the other basic human rights such as freedom of speech, but it does not need them to support or supplement its legitimacy. It is therefore not a luxury, a second-class right, a constitutional redundancy, or a subcategory of free speech, but the first liberty.

Religious liberty is fundamental for societies as well as for individuals, because it serves both as a protection for individual liberty and as a prerequisite for ordering the relationship of religion and public life. In today's world, pluralism makes religious liberty more necessary, just as religious liberty makes pluralism more likely, so that the First Amendment's wise ordering of liberty and diversity is now essential for freedom, justice, and civility.

Because freedom is a duty as well as a right, an obligation and not only an entitlement, all citizens in a free society are responsible for the rights of others just as others are responsible for theirs. Unless rights are exercised freely, and unless responsibilities are protected vigilantly, freedom, becoming empty, will be eroded.

In light of these fundamental principles, there are two reasons why religious liberty should rightly be seen as the first liberty. On the one hand, it comes first *logically*, in that it protects the inner freedom of thought, deliberation, judgment, and choice that is the source and subject of the later rights of free speech and free assembly. Though not infallible, conscience is inalienable. Thus, what we are each bound by according to the dictates of our reason and our conscience is the very deepest thing we also desire to speak of with freedom. And we further desire to gather together with others who prize those same things.

On the other hand, religious liberty comes first *historically*, in that it is only as religious liberty was guaranteed that the other rights were guaranteed, and it is only as religious liberty is guaranteed in the future that the other rights will remain protected, too. Religious liberty is therefore the precedent, pattern, and pledge for all other rights.

The Williamsburg Charter states that religious liberty is at once inalienable, foundational, and never subject to any court, and therefore stands as a searching challenge for any society claiming to be free: "A society is only as just and free as it is respectful of this right, especially toward the beliefs of its smallest minorities and least popular communities."

In Word and Deed

Such clarion principles are often dismissed today, or called on only to embellish patriotic themes with a rhetorical flourish. But for the revolutionary generation, they were anything but faded scribbles on parchment or a set of lofty quotations for monuments; they were woven into the warp and woof of the Revolution and a central secret of its success.

First, religious liberty was crucial to *winning freedom.* For a start, it was a distinct and powerful motive for the Revolution, as it had been since the beginning for many people coming to America. Read the founders, and the phrase "religious liberty and civil liberty" rolls off the tongue of the revolutionary generation as simply and naturally as "brother and sister"—and has done so throughout American history until the divorce of its components under duress in the current generation, when civil liberty has rashly been used to trump religious liberty.

Washington, for example wrote to the Reformed German congregation in New York in 1783, "The establishment of Civil and Religious Liberty was the Motive which induced me to the field."[20]

In addition, religious liberty was a powerful theme in the "Black Regiment," the group of pro-independence colonial preachers, garbed in black ministerial gowns, who were a key to justifying and inspiring the revolution. While some clergy opposed revolution, especially Anglicans, most others supported it wholeheartedly, particularly Congregationalists and

Baptists. Many not only preached on behalf of revolution but took an active role as chaplains and combatants. In Jefferson's tribute, "pulpit oratory ran like a shock of electricity through the whole colony."[21]

Yet another occasion when religious liberty and religion were accorded a crucial role in the Revolution was when the founders attributed the success of the Revolution to a clear sense of divine providence. Indeed, "the invisible hand" for Washington was not Adam Smith's free market but the hand of God in providence. "The hand of God has been so conspicuous in all this," he wrote to Brigadier General Nelson, "that he must be worse than an infidel that lacks faith, and more than wicked, that has not gratitude enough to acknowledge his obligations."[22]

Second, religious liberty was crucial to *ordering freedom.* The religious-liberty clauses, not the separation of powers, are the truly unique and revolutionary part of the Constitution. And they have proved not only distinctive but decisive in the American experiment. On the one hand, they are a sure protection of individual liberty—with the two clauses addressing different concerns but serving the same end: religious liberty. On the other hand, the religious-liberty clauses are a wise provision for ordering religion and public life, simultaneously addressing the demands of freedom, justice, and order, and allowing us to live with our deepest differences, so that diversity remains a source of strength rather than weakness.

Third, religious liberty was seen as crucial to *sustaining freedom.* Rightly protected and rightly ordered, religious liberty is the silent partner in the golden triangle of freedom. If religious liberty flourishes, then freedom, virtue, and faith all flourish, too; but without it, freedom, virtue, and faith are choked off at the roots, and the republic that they nourish withers, too.

Around the time that *Democracy in America* was published, Tocqueville told a friend how sad he was to see that in France religion, morality, and order were ranged in opposition to liberty and equality. This was deplorable because "the greatness and happiness of man in this world can only result from their union. Such, he said, was his basic idea, and where he had seen it best was in America.

Premarket Enterprise

The second feature of the First Amendment's ordering of religion and public life, and the resulting American settlement, was its astonishing unleashing of entrepreneurial vitality throughout American life. The point is often made that religion in America benefited from market forces; by mimicking free-market competition, it stayed free and unencumbered to spread its message and promote its causes.

The link is certainly close, but the point needs to be made with care, because the First Amendment preceded the spread of market capitalism by several decades. Scholars differ as to when market capitalism made serious inroads into the traditional agrarian world and its household economies, but in the United States it was certainly not as early as 1791, when the First Amendment passed and the separation of church and state was effected.

But the dynamics of the two forces are similar. By separating church and state—or, more properly, churches and states—the effect was the same as creating the open competition of a free market and a level playing field. Disestablishment, in this sense, was the equivalent of demonopolization, religious liberty for all was the equivalent of a level playing field, religious pluralism was the equivalent of open competition, and the premium placed on voluntary faith was the equivalent of the business opportunity opened up to the energetic and the hardworking.

The social result of the First Amendment was explosive. It liberated faith twice over—faith being understood, of course, to include the nontheistic and secular faiths, too. On the one hand, faith was freed from the insidious embrace of the state, and from its centuries-old dependence on the state, and thus from the laziness, lethargy, corruption, and control that came with it. Madison had argued for this from the beginning. Far from maintaining "the purity and efficacy" of faith, ecclesiastical establishments have had the contrary effect: "More or less in all places, pride and indolence in the Clergy; ignorance and servility in the laity; in both, superstition, bigotry, and persecution."[23]

On the other hand, faith was freed to be itself, and therefore freed to its own "free exercise." Faith could speak and act in society according to its own convictions and energies, and was limited only by its own resources and a proper consideration of the same right to the free exercise of others. The result was an astonishing release of religious entrepreneurialism that went hand in hand with the equally powerful democratic movement and changed the face of nineteenth-century America. In the opinion of the political scientist Robert Putnam, the faith communities became "the single most important repository of social capital in America."[24]

Among the lasting fruits of this premarket entrepreneurialism are the educational movement that saw the founding of many of the elite colleges and booster colleges, the reform movements that climaxed in the abolition of slavery, and the countless philanthropic initiatives that tackled the myriad needs of the poor and the oppressed.

Unquestionably, the American founders separated church and state, and equally unquestionably, the result was entirely positive. Curiously, however, there is a deep suspicion of the notion in some conservative circles today, a suspicion that goes far beyond a rejection of the extreme form of separation known as "separationism" or "strict separation." The latter, as we will see later, has serious flaws. It is not what the framers intended, and became influential only after World War II. But in reacting to separationism, many conservatives have gone overboard and are actually speaking against the separation of church and state.

One example is the common argument heard from the Religious Right that the separation of church and state is a "myth," that it was "not in the Constitution," and that it was an invention of Jefferson's through his reference to a "wall of separation" in his letter to the Danbury Baptists in 1802. A Republican congresswoman recently denounced the separation of church and state as a "lie."[25]

This argument is both wrong and foolish. The phrase is not in the Constitution, but the principle most certainly is. More important, both the framers and almost all Americans—certainly all Protestants—viewed the provision as principled and positive. Tocqueville went so far as to say that, as a Roman Catholic, he had met many priests and fellow Catholics who "assigned primary credit for the peaceful ascendancy of religion in their country to the separation of church and state."[26] Indeed, he added, he did not meet a single American in all his stay who thought otherwise.

Christian conservatives who are hesitant about the notion today should remember that the "separation" was originally a distinction rather than a divorce. Separation was not simply negative, a reaction to the evils and excesses of Constantine's hijacking of the mantle of the church. It was positive, a flower whose seed goes back to early American Baptists such as Roger Williams, who was the first to speak of "a wall of separation," and far earlier still to the teaching of Jesus about the different duties owed to "God" and to "Caesar," and then to a key succession of events and statements: the separation between emperor and pope when the emperor moved to Constantinople, the Fourth Treatise of Pope Gelasius in the fifth century (God "has separated the two offices for the time that followed, so that neither shall become proud"[27]), and later the clash between Pope Gregory VII and the Holy Roman Emperor Henry IV in the eleventh century.

In short, long before Jefferson and Madison spoke and wrote, the separation of church and state and its corollary of modern institutional pluralism had their beginnings in ideas that are basic to the Jewish and Christian faiths, though so far yet to be embraced by the other monotheistic faith, Islam.

Another example of a flawed understanding of the separation of church and state is George W. Bush's much-trumpeted but bungled policy of providing government money for what he calls "faith-based initiatives." Predictably, this initiative was surrounded by controversy from the start and did not live up to its supporters' hopes. At its best, it was a well-intentioned compliment to the dynamism of faith-based entrepreneurialism in the nineteenth century. The tribute was sincere and the intention laudable—to encourage the voluntarism and dynamic energy that are now recognized as the lifeblood of a healthy civil society, and to foster the little platoons and mediating institutions that are its cells.

But regardless of its political and legal problems, such as the accusations of cronyism and political manipulation, the project was self-defeating as a concept because the close relationship between government and faith-based groups almost inevitably leads, first, to a growing dependency of the faith-based organization on the government, and, eventually, to the effective secularization of the faith-based group. In the words of David Kuo, President George W. Bush's special assistant for faith-based initiatives, "Between Catholic Charities and Lutheran Social Services alone, for example, more than $1.5 billion went to faith-based groups every year. But their activity had come at a spiritual cost. They were, as organizations, largely secular."[28]

Early-nineteenth-century entrepreneurialism erupted precisely because faith was released from all governmental dependence; and today's entrepreneurialism will slowly wither as dependency on the government grows again. In other words, the core problem of the president's faith-based policy is not legal and constitutional but theological and spiritual. In the words of the nineteenth-century Catholic writer Félicité de Lamennais, "It was not with a cheque drawn on Caesar's bank that Jesus sent his apostles out into the world."[29]

Before being enticed back to the dangerous liaison that caused the church such problems in the past, leaders of the faith communities should heed Madison's warning and the lessons of the European experience and turn down the offer point-blank. (A recent Swedish study stated the European experience laconically: "Even the church is financed by the government, and the creation of even one non-profit philanthropic organization would be a quantum jump.")

True faith-based initiatives owe nothing to the government except its protection of their freedom to operate. They are freely chosen, voluntary activities that depend solely on their own believers and resources. As such they are never stronger than the strength of their own beliefs, the generosity of their own people, and the depth of their own resources and commitments—all without a single cent from the government's tempting purse or a triplicate form from the deadening hand of its bureaucracy.

Evangelicals, of all people, should be wary of government-supported faith-based initiatives, for they were the victims of earlier church-state establishments, the pioneers of the earlier entrepreneurialism as well as its principal beneficiaries—so much so that the nineteenth century in America was initially the Evangelical century and later the Protestant century. Yet the part that evangelicals played in the rise of the voluntary associations is often forgotten today, not least by evangelicals themselves, and by those who imagine that voluntary associations have been strong in America from the beginning.

Tocqueville stated the importance of voluntary associations clearly, but gave no background: "Whenever at the head of some new undertaking you see the government in France, or a man of rank in England, in the United States you will be sure to find an association."[30] His point is now taken up as if it had been true all along, and supporting quotations are easy to find. The United States, Max Weber observed, is the association-land par excellence. The American people, Max Lerner wrote, are a nation of joiners. Where two or three Americans are gathered together, James Luther Adams wrote, it is likely that a committee is being formed. All of which gave rise to H. L. Mencken's quip "Where two or three are gathered together and speaking of 'service,' you may be sure that someone is going to get 'gypped.'"

In fact, although the voluntary New England churches provide the seed principle of the voluntary associations, the associations' real rise came in Connecticut in the 1830s, as a direct result of the disestablishment of Congregationalism and in open imitation of William Wilberforce's Clapham Circle and their success in the abolition of slavery and the reformation of moral standards in England.

Lyman Beecher, along with his fellow evangelical Leonard Bacon the architects of the movement, admitted he had originally been a diehard supporter of the established church in Connecticut. Thus, disestablishment day, he wrote, was "as dark a day as ever I saw.... The injury done to the cause of Christ, we then supposed, was irreparable." But it turned out to be the opposite: *"the best thing that ever happened to the State of Connecticut* [Beecher's italics]. It cut the churches loose from dependence on state support. It threw them wholly on their own resources and on God."[31]

The net result of disestablishment was gain, not loss. "They say ministers have lost their influence," Beecher said. "The fact is, that they have gained.... The Protestantism of the Old World is still fettered by the union of the Church with the State."[32]

Premarket, or free-market, entrepreneurialism is the direct outcome of the separation of church and state, and the perfect expression of the marriage between faith, freedom, and diversity. Thanks to the First Amendment, nothing comes closer to the secret of the genius of American vitality, and Americans who care about liberty and a healthy civil society need to rescue its brilliance and constructive generosity from the clash and din of the culture wars and from the well-intentioned efforts of those who do not understand its genius.

No Rivers of Blood Here

The third feature of the First Amendment's ordering of religion and public life, and of the unwritten American settlement, is the robust social harmony it has created. Many Americans I have met know their system so well that they take it for granted, and it takes the fresh eyes of a visitor to appreciate what the founders achieved. But if contrast is the mother of clarity, the founders were only too aware of the dismal history that was the dark backdrop to their endeavors—summarized in Roger Williams's term "torrents of blood" and Madison's "rivers of blood."

The horizon of the founders' discussion was the egregious religious evils of history, such as the Inquisition, the slaughter of the Albigensians, and the religious wars of the seventeenth century. The backdrop to ours today is the even more horrific secularist evils, such as the Jacobin massacre of the Vendée in 1793, Stalin's Ukrainian terror famine in the 1930s, Mao's Cultural Revolution in the 1950s, and Pol Pot's killing fields in Cambodia in the 1970s. In both cases, the black record of man's inhumanity to man, especially in its state-sponsored forms, provides the contrast for why the founders fought for religious liberty in America, passed the Bill of Rights that protected it, and worked out what it meant to live "with liberty and justice for all."

We dare not allow those six words to become abstract or ceremonial. The way I pay tribute to the founders' brilliance is this: when the American settlement worked, as it mostly has, it not only fostered liberty and justice for all, *it created a society in which strong religious convictions and strong political civility could go hand in hand.* Most societies have one or the other of these two forces, but rarely both of them together, and it was the crowning genius of the American founders to achieve that feat, and to do so in a society that from the beginning was highly diverse and highly vocal in its opinions and its demands.

There are many parts of the world that have one or other of these two forces. That is not unusual. President Hu Jintao of China for example, correctly trumpets his notion of a "harmonious society." But with a Leninist one-party state, harmony without liberty is another word for tyranny.

Or again, Western Europe has been characterized for most of the last fifty years by strong political civility over religion and public life. There were obvious exceptions to the overall picture, such as the "troubles" between Protestants and Catholics in Ulster; and I would have to add "until recently," because the general picture has now been upset by the so-called reverse colonization and the massive influx of new immigrants into Europe, especially Muslims.

But anyone who knows Europe realizes that whatever peaceable attitude there was, was only a modest achievement, because in a deeply secular Europe there was little religion about which to be uncivil. Churchgoing in Sweden, for example, had dipped as low as 3 percent; in the upper Midwest of the United States, by contrast, where Swedes and other Scandinavians have settled in large numbers, churchgoing has long been well above the American average.

Religiously speaking, America looks like the lush, warm tropics where every exotic form of spirituality grows in extravagant profusion. European religion, by contrast, looks and feels like the Arctic, and the chilly climate of state-sponsored secularity is not conducive to outdoor contests, let alone clashes, between faiths.

In the Middle East and elsewhere, the opposite problem is apparent—passionate, overheated religious convictions with no political civility to match. As a result, and as our television screens and newspaper headlines tell us daily, there is little civility, even less liberty, and all too commonly no respect for life.

The genius of the American way is that, on the whole, it has given full expression to religious liberty for people of all faiths, while at the same time doing so in a way that fosters political civility as well as allows the "free exercise" of strong religious convictions.

Needless to say, the culture wars are evidence enough that the earlier settlement has broken down, and with it the place of religious liberty in public life has again become controversial. In the next chapters we will analyze why this has happened and then propose a constructive way forward. But first we need to understand and appreciate what the First Amendment once achieved and what is at stake for the future.

As I have argued, religious liberty is not just for the religious, and it is not just a private matter. It is a public matter and a national matter, and it is as crucial for secularists and those with "no faith" (the so-called religious nones whose faith is naturalistic) as it is for those with religious faith. The freedom that religious liberty promotes and protects is powerful and precious for individuals, but the provisions it offers for ordering public life lie at the very heart of the genius of the United States, and will need to remain so if a free people are to have a chance of remaining free forever.

Chapter Three

The Broken Settlement

Ireland, the land of my fathers, has recently been edging toward the side of the angels, though for long, sad centuries the pages of Irish history have been stained with all the blood and tears shed over religion and national life. So much so that when the Irish could cry no more, they turned their emotions into black humor and mocked the bitter prejudices that hurt them—with wry jokes such as the story of the Israeli visitor to Ulster being asked at gunpoint, "A Jew, yes. But are you a Catholic Jew or a Protestant Jew?" Or the airline steward announcing over the loudspeaker as a plane flew into Ulster, "The temperature in Belfast is 65 degrees, and please put your watches back three hundred years."

Only those who have suffered, it is said, have a right to turn such dark humor on themselves, and certainly the story of sectarian violence and its place in modern inhumanity is no laughing matter for the rest of the world. But as we saw in the first chapter, the challenge of living with our deep differences, and of making the world safe for diversity, is one of the greatest tasks we face in the global era.

Out of Many, One

Grappling with liberty, diversity, and unity has been part and parcel of the United States's being the world's "first new nation." Indeed, E Pluribus Unum, or "Out of Many, One," is not just the American motto but one of America's great accomplishments. Whereas the special pride of the ancient Jews was that out of one—namely, Abraham—they had become many, the special pride of Americans is that out of many— namely, the diverse tide of settlers and immigrants—they have become one.

No feat could be more relevant to the world in the global era, for on a small planet united by our communications, our travel, our markets, and our common planetary problems, we are still divided by our religions, our political ideologies, our cultures, and our civilizations. There will not be, and there should not be, a universal way of being modern. Multiple modernities are both inevitable and proper, but the world requires precedents and patterns for how the challenge of living with our differences may be tackled, and the American experiment provides the most thought through and helpful model so far.

The questions raised are daunting. How can we live with our deepest differences on a global scale? How do we do it when there are tensions between *entire ways of life*, some of which are grounded in truth claims that are *absolute*—ways of life that are so different as to be philosophically and socially incompatible? What does it take in such a setting to establish a global public square that is both *cosmopolitan and civil*, doing justice to both halves of the first word—so that in some sense we are citizens of the worldwide "cosmos" while also citizens of our local city or "polis"? And how can we build such a worldwide order that promotes liberty, justice, and equal opportunity for all while allowing for the full consideration of global diversity and disorder? And above all, how can we do so when the differences that are the deepest differences of all are religiously and ideologically grounded differences, over which humans have fought and are still fighting?

John Kennedy's call for "a world safe for diversity" was delivered at American University in 1963 under the shadow of the Soviet nuclear threat. It is even more relevant in the face of today's challenges of exploding religious pluralism. The president's phrase is sometimes dismissed with a snort, however, because of its echo of Woodrow Wilson's call for "a world safe for democracy." As has frequently been remarked, the call for "a world safe for democracy" led to "a world safe for dictatorship," and "the war to end all wars" led to "a peace to end all peace."

The issue, however, is too important to be left to cynics, if only because not to try for a constructive answer reinforces the chances of a destructive answer, and of the continuance of today's failing and outdated policies. A naive answer will certainly produce unintended consequences, but a constructive answer that attempts to be self-critical at least opens the discussion of an issue we cannot avoid in the global era: forging a global public square for the common discussion of our common problems in a world with deep and important differences.

The American settlement we looked at in the last chapter might well have been one model for the world to consider. But ironically, as I said, at the very moment when many countries in the world have moved beyond their traditional stage of homogeneous societies and are ready to appreciate the challenges and lessons of American liberty and pluralism, a generation of culture warring has called America's earlier success into question and cast doubt over the relevance of the founders' provision for America, let alone for the world.

The problem is not unique to the United States. All three of the principal Western settlements of religion and public life are in crisis and need to be reordered. They have each been called into question by the new realities of the global age—the French mainly because of the influx of Muslim immigrants whose stubbornly nonprivatized faith and ways of life are an open defiance of French secularism, the English because the even more varied influx of Commonwealth immigrants of many religions has shown both the minority status and the feeble spiritual condition of the still-established Church of England, and the American because of trends that have upset the earlier settlement and thrown the founders' provisions into the mixing bowl.

In all three cases, the point is not to lament the collapse of the previous settlement but to view the challenge to change as a catalyst rather than a crisis, and therefore a task for the West as much as for the new immigrants, with the aim of applying enduring Western principles to new circumstances so that we create a new and constructive settlement for our time—recognizing, of course, that all nations share the same overall challenge today, and that the stakes for democratic nations are higher than ever.

Am I proposing a single, procrustean solution for all three countries? No. France, England, and the United States (and Australia, Canada, and other Western countries that face the same challenge) all have their own distinctive histories and cultures, and need to construct their own solutions, though learning from the experience of the others. Am I about to propose a solution for the United States that challenges the founding principles of the American republic? On the contrary, I could well argue that Americans themselves are doing that. But what I would argue is that the proposal to forge "a cosmopolitan and civil public square" does better justice to the founders' principles than either of the two positions now battling in American public life.

In other words, the problems that led to the breakdown of the earlier settlement do not mean that the founders' principles are wrong or outdated. Rather, the problems show where the foundational principles need to be renegotiated under modern conditions so that their original purpose may still be fulfilled—perhaps on an even broader world stage, should other nations care to heed the American lessons.

In the same way, it is a mistake to view the increasing diversity of religions in Europe simply as an expansion of consumer *choice,* as if the problem and the solution could be reduced to economic dimensions and rational choice calculations. (Though there is no question that consumerism sometimes adds to the controversies—for example, the report of a well-meaning Tokyo department store that included among its Christmas decorations a Santa Claus nailed to a cross.[1]) Instead, the problem should be seen as the emergence of a political and cultural *challenge* to democratic first principles, a mutual challenge both to Europe and to religions such as Islam to confront the dilemmas of free and just societies that value both liberty and diversity.

Exploding Pluralism

What are the changes that have called the earlier American settlement into question? The first is an explosion of pluralism in which the United States both leads and finds itself linked to the world. Pluralism is obviously no stranger to the American experience, and it is a vital partner in the development of American religious liberty. As we saw, pluralism makes religious liberty more necessary, just as religious liberty makes pluralism more likely. Voltaire's remark about England is magnified greatly in the United States: "If one religion only were allowed in England, the government would very possibly become arbitrary; if there were but two, the people would cut one another's throats. But there are such a multitude, they all live happy and in peace."[2]

The very story of America is the story of an ever-expanding pluralism. If the middle colonies in the eighteenth century were one of the most pluralistic regions of the earth, the pluralism was largely Protestant. With the arrival of Roman Catholics, it became a Christian pluralism, then a Jewish and Christian pluralism, and then a loosely biblical pluralism—in the sense that the diverse new and "made in America" religions of the nineteenth century, such as Mormonism, although they were not Christian in any orthodox sense, still owed their provenance to the Bible rather than to the Koran, the Bhagavad Gita, or the Pali canon.

After World War II, the 1950s predominance of "the Protestant-Catholic-Jew" understanding marked a clear watershed. And since then, the growth in pluralism has accelerated again—in two directions. First, American pluralism now includes sizable numbers of all the world's religions, Buddhists and Muslims in particular. Second, the pluralism now goes beyond religion altogether to include a growing number of Americans with no religious preference at all. These secularists, or so-called religious nones, were once about 2 percent of Americans but are now around 9 to 11 percent, and significantly stronger in the Pacific Northwest and among the educated elites.[3]

The explosion of pluralism is a social and historical fact that should be a simple matter to acknowledge. Its effects can be seen in the demographic makeup of contemporary American society. The state of California, for example, has America's most diverse as well as its largest population. It accepts almost a third of the world's immigrants and represents today what New York did a hundred years ago—the point of entry for millions of new Americans.[4] It is a "minority majority" state with a remarkable mix of the diverse cultures of Europe, Latin America, Africa, Asia, and the Middle East.

To be sure, it is one thing to acknowledge this new pluralism and another to adjust to it. But the problem is compounded further by two inadequate responses to it. On the liberal side, many have talked airily of "diversity" but have not taken in the fact that pluralism means a diversity of complete ways of life and not just of worldviews—ways of life, that is, with their religious, cultural, and historical baggage firmly attached that cannot and should not be shed at the frontier posts of public life. All too often liberalism has been the champion of a diversity that is abstract, ethereal, and unhistorical, the constant enemy of real-life diversity with all its messiness.

On the conservative side, many supporters of the Religious Right have responded badly by confusing *pluralism* with *relativism*. The former is simply a social fact that is undeniable— "everyone is now everywhere," it is said with some exaggeration of the modern diversity of religious, ethnic, and social differences—whereas the latter is a philosophical conclusion that follows for some but not for others. Because pluralism does not necessarily entail relativism, it would be quite legitimate to distinguish between the two, acknowledge the first, and oppose the second. But by confusing the two, opponents of pluralism-as-relativism oppose the facts and act defiantly as if pluralism had not changed the game as it has.

This confusion has long bedeviled discussions of official prayer in public schools, and supporters of school prayer have found themselves on the horns of a dilemma of their own choosing. Insisting on official Christian prayer in such pluralistic settings, they either ignore the diversity and pray as if everyone shared their faith—thus *scandalizing* those who do not; or they respect the diversity and pray in an in-offensive way that tries to appeal to as many faiths as possible—thus *secularizing* their own faith while still offending those who reject public prayer of any kind. The infamous New York Regents' Prayer, it should be remembered, was written by lawyers, not people of faith at all.

Whose prayer is to be prayed, and how? Should those who insist on praying scandalize others or secularize themselves? The practical dilemma of prayer in pluralistic public schools came home to me many years ago when I spoke to a father who had just moved to Utah along with his wife and teenage son. As a Southern Baptist in Georgia, he had never been able to see what all the fuss was about when Jewish parents complained about their children being the odd ones out in a southern classroom full of Baptists. Suddenly his son had found himself the sole Baptist among Mormons, and he in turn found himself objecting to Mormon prayers in the public school and realized for the first time what it must have been like to be a Jew among Baptists.

The founders' first principles of religious liberty can of course be applied to school prayer in several ways. For example, the golden rule of equal liberty for all could be applied to school prayer as "One in, all in" and respected by praying a different prayer every day of the school month—Christian one day, Jewish the next, Muslim after that, then Buddhist, Hindu, Mormon, Scientologist, Wiccan, and so on, until all the faiths in the school are covered. Such a policy would surely lead to chaos and indifference rather than tolerance, a misguided illustration of the old adage that "comparative religion makes people comparatively religious."

The alternative application of the golden rule would be to say, "One out, all out," and to conclude—I think rightly, for religious even more than constitutional reasons—that public schools are not the place to have official teacher-led prayer, Christian or otherwise. A moment of silence, perhaps; and freedom to pray alone at any time; and freedom to pray in student-initiated groups after school hours, certainly; but not official prayer in public schools when contemporary levels of the social fact of pluralism mean that the principle of religious liberty for all is contravened. (As all these "equal access" freedoms show, it is a perverse myth that "children are not allowed to pray in public schools.")

If the contemporary levels of American pluralism have raised the bar in working out what religious liberty now means, imagine the challenge of worldwide pluralism. At least the United States has lived with the challenges of liberty and diversity for two hundred years. Many European countries, by contrast, have moved from traditional homogeneity to modern diversity in a few years, only to find that the precedent and pattern America once offered no longer seems to be working for Americans.

Put differently, countries such as Britain, France, Germany, and the Netherlands, which are now wrestling with the problems of diversity, have never had to have a powerful tradition of working out what religious liberty means, and have never needed myths of assimilation such as "Americanization." But the country with the richest first principles and the most powerful myths is no longer acting as a model, let alone as Winthrop's "city upon a hill" or Pericles' "school to the world."

Expanding Statism

The second change that has thrown the earlier settlement into the mixer is the enormous expansion of the state in relation to the church. "Church and state" is a shorthand phrase that obscures as much as it illuminates, and in America it is often triply misleading because it suggests that there is a single church, a single state, and a simple and clear distinction between the two. In America's federal system, of course, there were churches and states from the beginning, and now there are faith communities of all sorts. And the problem is compounded further, for, as Harold Berman, dean of American scholars on law and religion, points out, the framers spoke more of "religion and government" than of "church and state."

But when all the definitions and distinctions have been clarified, a crucial fact emerges clearer than ever. Not only have religion and government each changed over the course of two hundred years, but the relationship between them has also changed. What has happened, in Berman's words, is a complete "exchange of roles."

In the 1780s religion played a primary role in social life ... and government played a relatively minor, though necessary, supportive role, whereas in the 1980s religion plays a relatively minor, though necessary, supportive role and government plays a primary role. On the other hand, the role played by government in the social life of America in the 1780s (and for almost a century and a half thereafter) was openly and strongly influenced and directed by religion, whereas in the 1980s that is much less true and in many respects not true at all, while the role played by religion in the social life of America in the 1980s is openly and strongly influenced and directed by government.[5]

When the First Amendment passed, Berman concludes, government was "the handmaid of religion," whereas today religion is "the handmaid of government."[6]

Not surprisingly, such a colossal reversal has sent out reverberations to every level of church-state relations—whether constitutional interpretation, volunteerism in public life, or religious liberty itself. And with the growth of the modern bureaucratic surveillance state, the problem of state encroachment is only going to get worse. Thus the warning must be clear. As the Williamsburg Charter states: "Less dramatic but also lethal to freedom and the chief menace to religious liberty today is the expanding power of government control over personal behavior and the institutions of society, when the government acts not so much in deliberate hostility to, but in reckless disregard of, communal belief and personal conscience."[7]

Emerging Separationism

The third change that has thrown the earlier settlement into the mixer is a new and more stringent form of the notion of the separation of church and state. As we saw earlier, the First Amendment's provision that separates church and state is the most distinctive and decisive part of the U.S. Constitution. The words may not be in the Constitution, but the idea most certainly is, and the force of its positive contribution was accepted almost universally in the early republic, even by Roman Catholics, whose church had sternly denounced the idea elsewhere. More recently, of course, the Second Vatican Council embraced it.

Yet while the framers clearly separated the institutions of church and state, they never separated the relationship of religion and government; which means that their separation was anything but absolute. Part of the reason was that there was no one, clear, and agreed pattern in mind from the outset. As historians have pointed out, the framers had no single pattern of church-state separation in mind when they went into the Constitutional Convention, and they had no single pattern in mind when they came out. There were then, and there will always be, alternative ways to interpret the Constitution, different views that have a life of their own and that will wax and wane over the generations.

Having said that, there is no question that the predominant view of the founders was what today would be called "accommodating." What it might have lacked in strict logical and legal consistency, it made up for in prudence and goodwill. The separation of church and state meant a clear distinction between the two, but by no means did it mean a divorce. Behind this broad tolerance lay the founders' general agreement on what I call the "golden triangle of freedom" (freedom requires virtue; virtue requires faith of some sort; faith requires freedom; and so on) and therefore on the fundamental importance of religious liberty to public life. The provisions for religion in the Northwest Ordinance, the appointment of chaplains in the

House and Senate, and the repeated calls for days of prayer and fasting by various presidents were the practical outworking of such views.

At the storm center of the modern debate stands Thomas Jefferson and his advocacy of "a wall of separation between Church and State," the famous words he wrote to the Danbury Baptist Association on New Year's Day 1802. The metaphor of the wall was first used by Roger Williams, and when we ask what Jefferson meant, it is important to set his statement in the context of his whole life and practice, especially at the time he wrote the words.

Earlier, Jefferson had been more openly deist and anti-religious, but two things had changed by the time he wrote the letter. On the one hand, he had read Joseph Priestley's *A History of the Corruptions of Christianity* in the early 1790s. After this he softened his earlier views and saw himself as an adherent of an uncorrupted faith—loosely approximating Unitarianism. On the other hand, as his altered position on faith coincided with his presidency, he shifted to a view of religion and public life that some see as utilitarian and others as hypocritical. But whatever his motive, and whatever the gap between his private and public views, his public view came closer to that of the other framers and to a view of faith that was vital to freedom. "The Christian religion," he wrote in 1801, "when brought to the original purity and simplicity of its original institutor, is a religion of all others most friendly to liberty."[8]

Thus Jefferson advocated a stricter view of separation than many of the other founders, but his "wall of separation" bears no resemblance to that of his contemporary supporters whose views lack the subtlety of the sage of Charlottesville. For some of the framers, such a view was unquestionably utilitarian, and even a bit cynical. But it was not necessarily hypocritical. And it was this functional appreciation of faith that lay behind several incidents for which Jefferson and the other framers have been charged with hypocrisy—for instance, the story Ethan Allen told of a friend meeting President Jefferson on his way to church one Sunday "with his large red prayer book under his arm" and exchanging greetings.

"Which way are you walking, Mr. Jefferson?" the friend asked.

"To church, Sir," the president replied.

"You going to church, Mr. J.? You do not believe a word in it."

"Sir," said Mr. Jefferson, "no nation has ever yet existed or been governed without religion. Nor can be. The Christian religion is the best religion that has ever been given to man, and I as chief Magistrate of this nation am bound to give it the sanction of my example. Good morning, Sir."[9]

Jefferson's example is instructive. In two important areas, there was a striking gap between his private and public views—over slavery and over religion in public life. In the case of slavery, it is hard not to conclude that the writer of the Declaration of the Independence was hypocritical. He owned more than three hundred slaves in his lifetime, he had more when he died than when he wrote the Declaration, and he imported slaves into France, although he knew that slavery was illegal there and not customary as it was in Virginia. But beyond his vested interest in his own slaves, there was always his anguish over the unavoidable dilemma he saw: the slaves' freedom would endanger America's freedom. In his own words, he was caught between "justice in one scale, and self-preservation in the other."[10]

In the case of religion in public life, Jefferson was probably not so much hypocritical or anguished as utilitarian and savvy. He was a deist who undoubtedly loathed organized religion and serious theology of all kinds—Protestant, Catholic, and Jewish. He believed that the Christian faith had been seriously corrupted and would soon be replaced by Unitarianism, and he was a church-state separationist who fiercely defended his "wall of separation." Yet as the conversation with Ethan Allen shows, whether Jefferson was two-faced or simply utilitarian, there is no question that he also believed that freedom requires virtue, and virtue faith, and that he as "chief Magistrate" must support certain public expressions of faith.

The fact is that the largest regular meetings for worship in America during Jefferson's presidency were under the roof of the U.S. Capitol, and with Jefferson present and supplying the music through the Marine Band.

In other words, Jefferson declared his position on the "wall of separation," but he also demonstrated what he intended, and his deeds are as important as his words. In a day before politicians and pundits talked constantly of "sending signals," Jefferson's signals were clear. On New Year's Day, Friday, January 1, 1802, he wrote to the Danbury Baptists about the "wall of separation," and in line with that, he refused to have "fastings and thanksgivings as my predecessors did."[11] But only two days later, the very same weekend, on Sunday, January 3, he as the chief executive went to a worship service in the "Hall" of the House of Representatives, and did so regularly for the next seven years. One contemporary said that the president "constantly attended public worship in the Hall," usually arriving on horseback and once braving heavy rain to get there in time.[12]

Beyond any doubt, church services in the Capitol in Jefferson's day were as common and uncontroversial as they were popular. A veritable potpourri of preachers and churches passed through when Jefferson was present, many of them unabashedly evangelical and even evangelistic; and money for religious purposes was raised openly and often in the Capitol, with the president himself donating.

More startlingly still for someone later cited as the advocate of a "strict separation" between government and religion, Jefferson allowed religious services in executive-branch buildings. Episcopalians regularly used the War Office and Baptists the Treasury. James Hutson of the Library of Congress describes these services in the executive buildings as even more "religious" than those in the Capitol because they included the celebration of sacraments that was absent from those in the latter. His conclusion of a broad survey of worship in government buildings in Jefferson's time is blunt: "It is no exaggeration to say that, on Sundays, in Washington during Thomas Jefferson's presidency, the state became the church."[13]

The point is of more than antiquarian interest. Hutson describes Jefferson's approach as "a carefully balanced strategy of words and action to convey his policy on church and state to his fellow citizens."[14] Neither he nor the government would ever be a party to any imposed and uniform belief or exercise. Let there be no doubt about that. But Jefferson was fully supportive, as being in the public interest, of "voluntary, non-discriminatory religious activity, including church services, by putting at its disposal public property, public facilities, and public personnel, including the president himself."[15]

Neither *nuanced* nor *carefully balanced* would be the words to describe the views of many who cite Jefferson today. His words have been torn from his deeds, his metaphor has been made into a myth, what he expressed privately has been forced out into public policy, and his "wall of separation" has become canonical for the school of constitutional interpretation known as *separationism,* or the strict, total, and absolute separation of church and state. Powerfully argued by Leo Pfeffer and a group of Jews, Baptists, and secularists, separationism first triumphed in the case of *Everson v. Board of Education* in 1947 and has since become one of the two leading positions in the subsequent battles over interpreting the Constitution.

In the process, the simple metaphor used by Roger Williams and Thomas Jefferson has been inflated, reiterated, and elevated until it has become both a comprehensive theory and a battle cry. For many, it has effectively replaced the actual text of the Constitution itself. Sweeping, rigid interpreters of the No Establishment clause, supporters of strict separationism argue that public life should be inviolably secular and all expressions of religious life should be inviolably private. In the words of Justice Wiley Rutledge in 1947, "We have staked the very existence of our country on the faith that complete separation between state and religion is best for the state and best for religion." Justice Hugo Black argued similarly, "The wall must be kept high and impregnable. We could not approve the slightest breach"—ignoring the plain historical fact that Jefferson's wall of separation was as characteristically porous; or better still, it was as serpentine and wavy as the walls of his beloved "ackademical village," the University of Virginia.[16]

My point here is not to dispute the notion of the "strict separation" of church and state or to advocate the practices that Jefferson followed so consistently. I wish only to underscore two consequences for our unfolding story. First, modern separationism, as the sharp contrast with Jefferson shows, is a decisive break with both the understanding of the founders and the informal American settlement that lasted from 1791 to the post–World War II era. Second, modern separationism clearly carries consequences for the relationship of faith and freedom that the founders saw as essential for sustaining republican freedom. What those consequences are, and what they mean for sustainable freedom, must also be brought into the discussion.

One overall conclusion is plain: under the weight of the combined impact of exploding pluralism, the expansion of the state, and emerging separationism, the early American settlement, so brilliantly described by Tocqueville, is gone, and gone for good. So it is not enough merely to describe or to celebrate the earlier American settlement. Even at its best, it was always a matter of "for better or worse," and the dark needs to be acknowledged along with the bright.

Yet the earlier settlement has gone, and in its place we have the bitterness and acrimony of the culture wars. But these, too, have their silver lining, for the crisis they represent is a usable crisis, just as the past that they try to bury is a usable past. What matters is not to lament the past but to address the crisis in light of the enduring American principles that are the best of the past, and to do so in a way that simultaneously demonstrates America's answer for herself as well as one possible answer for the global age and its immense new challenges.

Chapter Four

Say No to the Sacred Public Square

Some years ago, I had the privilege of addressing a forum of Chinese CEOs in the business school of one of China's most prestigious universities. It was an official occasion, and there was a long and somewhat tedious program that included the singing of the Communist Party anthem and the cutting of a gigantic birthday cake for the party. But after all that had gone on, I was surprised at the intensity with which people listened as I spoke, and then engaged in a spirited discussion. But the most searching question of the day was raised at the end by the dean.

"What am I missing?" the dean asked. "We in China are fascinated by the Christian roots of the Western past, in order to see what we can learn for China's future. But you in the West are cutting yourself off from your roots. What am I missing?"

The dean's question was apt, because I have been in many conversations in China that have run something like this: "The

Communist Party in China is in power, but as everyone knows without saying so publicly, the communist ideology is hollow and incapable of guiding China as she reemerges onto the world stage as a superpower. But what will be the philosophy/ethic/faith/ideology capable of guiding China as she faces her supreme challenge: opening up the economy and liberalizing political and cultural institutions without creating chaos? Will the new faith be a form of authoritarianism, a revived Confucianism or Buddhism, a Chinese materialism, or could it be the Christian faith, which has grown so rapidly in the last generation and could one day be the majority faith in China?"[1]

This is not the place to debate the future of China or the "gifts" of the Jewish and Christian faiths to Western civilization—though among those discussed as either direct or indirect contributions are the distinctive Western culture of giving and caring, the recurring Western impulse toward movements of reform, the rise of the universities, the flowering of modern science, the explosion of capitalism and modern democracy, and the emergence of human rights.

Along with such gifts that are civilization-wide, each Western country has its own legacy of distinctive features that it owes at least in part to the Jewish and Christian faiths. The American settlement, for example, owes its notion of constitutionalism to the Jewish understanding of covenant and its earliest notions of freedom of conscience to Protestant dissenters such as Roger Williams and William Penn.

If this is broadly the case, the dean's question is even more important for the West than for China. There are no intellectual property rights or patents on the great ideas that shape civilization, but at the same time no great civilization endures if it cuts its ties to whatever is the source of its greatness. So what will happen to the West and to individual countries in the West if they sever their Jewish and Christian roots decisively and forever?

There are three broad answers to this question. One possibility is that there will be a *transposition;* that is, to use a musical analogy, a country or civilization may transpose its central ideas from one key to another. For example, human rights were first composed and sung in a distinctively Jewish and Christian key: human dignity was inalienable because human beings were "created in the image of God." This motive is stunningly clear in the work of William Wilberforce, the greatest social reformer of all time and the forerunner of the human-rights revolution, who fought for the abolition of the slave trade in 1807 and of slavery itself in 1833 under the banner of rehumanizing African slaves ("Am I not a man and a brother?"). Conceivably, human rights that began this way could be transposed into a purely secular key, and many argue that such a shift is well under way today.

A second possible outcome is *decline;* that is, again using a musical analogy, no other key is capable of sustaining the music well. Or to change the image: the life of cut flowers is shorter than the life of living plants. Again for example, there are signs that the laudable secular passion for human rights finds itself in open contradiction with some of the ideas about humanness put forward by fellow secularists. Consider the much-trumpeted claims by the Princeton professor Peter Singer that humans are not essentially different from animals, so that human rights are a form of ungrounded species chauvinism and should be repudiated along with other prejudices such as ethnocentrism.

How are such objections to be answered within the secularist framework? Are human rights only a secular parroting of Jewish and Christian views of human uniqueness? It will not do to proclaim human rights louder and louder, and yet have no grounds for them. Not only would that sound irrational, superstitious, and all too much like a secular fundamentalism; it would play into the hands of the strongest critics. For certain objectors both inside and outside the West now argue that "human rights" are only a late-Enlightenment Western ideology—high-sounding ideals that are the weapons with which the West promotes its power agenda. And many nations have grown wary of "human-rights imperialism," suspicious that "human rights" are a spurious excuse for "transnational interference" in the affairs of sovereign states. In such a skeptical climate, cut-flower rights-without-roots will eventually wither as ideals that are hollow, meddlesome, and open to abuse—while real human rights will suffer in practice after they have been weakened in theory, and at the hands of democrats rather than tyrants.

A third possible outcome is *renewal;* that is, there can be a spiritual renewal of the beliefs that are at the root of Western civilization, parallel to the political and civic renewal of which the founders wrote. George Mason wrote of "a frequent recurrence to fundamental principles," and Jefferson of "a revolution every twenty years."[2] Curiously, this possibility reflects the interesting parallel between the founders' view of the cycle of political freedom and their Jewish and Puritan forebears' view of the cycle of spiritual vitality, with the former being a secularization of the latter.

What the *exodus* was for the Jews and *conversion* was spiritually for the Puritans, *revolution* was politically for the founders. Similarly, what *covenant* was for both the Jews and the Puritans, *constitution* was for the founders. And what *return* was for the Jew and *revival* was for the Puritans, Mason's "frequent recurrence" and Jefferson's "revolution every twenty years" were for the founders.

For all of them, history is linear and not cyclical, as it was for the Greeks and Romans. So the future is never a rerun of the past. But the best way forward is partly to go back, so that the remembered past is the key to a renewed future, and a usable past is a liberal force rather than being purely conservative, let alone reactionary or antiquarian.

The Fall of Public Man

Can there be a renewal of the first principles of the American settlement that satisfies the challenges and changed conditions of our times? Is it realistic to conceive of forging a vision of the public square that does full justice to the extravagant demands of modern liberty as well as the exacting demands of modern diversity? I believe there can be, and that such a renewal may truly be the last best hope for the American experiment. For the question confronting the United States is whether a constructive solution can be found to the culture warring over religion and public life, a solution that is recognized as being in the interests of Americans of all faiths and no faith, or whether the culture wars will be fought to the finish at whatever cost to freedom of such a Pyrrhic victory.

Beyond any doubt, the United States in the last generation has suffered a serious breakdown in public civility that is the result of an even more serious decline in the quality of American common life. The very idea of a common life and the sense that there are public matters that are common property to all Americans sounds increasingly quaint or naive in the stormy climate of the culture wars.

The symptoms of the collapse of public life are widespread and include a long list of broader developments: the disappearance of urban public space, the shrinking of a book-and-newspaper-reading public, the growth of gated communities and constant surveillance, the rise of political primaries and the weakening of political parties, the decline of elections into public-relations contests, the degradation of political deliberation and debate into culture warring, the dominance of television as a source of news and of entertainment and of profit as the priority in television, the growing resort to referendums at the expense of legislatures, the precipitous collapse of trust and voter participation, the rise of political dynasties and celebrity candidates, the expansion of lobbies and lobbyists, the increase of cronyism and corruption, the appearance of billionaire politicians and of the mounting power of money as the loudest voice in America, and the exponential growth of secrecy and classified documents.

In short, the 1960s cry for more participatory politics has led to less participation in politics, and the call for greater majority rule has led to greater influence for minorities. Overall, the fall of public man confronts American democracy with a blunt question: What would American citizens think if they were actually encouraged to think for themselves as democracy assumes?

The journalist Fareed Zakaria has described the broad outcome of these trends as an excess of democracy, and in a nonrepublican direction that the founders would have feared: "There can be such a thing as too much democracy—too much of an emphatically good thing."[3] For our purposes, what matters is a general collapse of the American public philosophy, or common vision of the common good; and in its wake the stok-

ing up of the culture wars, and in particular the endless conflict over the proper place of faiths in public life. A grand
confusion now reigns as to any guiding principles by which
people of different faiths may enter the public square and engage with each other robustly but civilly. The incoherence of recent court decisions has only made the problem worse.

The result is the holy-war front of America's wider culture
wars. Disputes over religion and politics in the last two decades have been bitterly polarized, extremes have surfaced
regularly, resort to law has become reflexive, and opponents
with no arguments left have kept on trading tired insults and
launching endless lawsuits. We are now at the point where
no issue is too insignificant to spark a new attack, and no
end is in sight to the number of possible lawsuits that may be
launched or conflagrations set ablaze.

"We will always win in the end," a leader of the American
Civil Liberties Union told me in the 1980s, "simply because
we have more lawyers than anyone else." But that is no longer the case. The other side has grown wise to the tactic, so
that batteries of lawyers now match batteries of lawyers, and
defense funds defense funds, and the prospects of potential
litigation stretch to the horizon and beyond. Just as America
has allowed the free market to erode the bonds of social co-
hesion and filled the vacuum with lawyers, litigation, and
prisons, so America has grown careless about the arts of political civility and compromise and filled the vacuum with
lawyers, litigation, and the culture wars.

Self-Fulfilling Strife

I made clear in the first chapter that many of the issues dividing the two sides are substantive, critical, and fully worthy

of democratic debate. They are issues on which all responsible citizens should take a position, and issues that will be decisive for the republic. Not for one moment am I advocating any stifling of the issues or a helicopter politics that hovers above the issues and never lands. At stake in the resolution of passionate issues such as abortion and same-sex marriage are competing views of the freedom, justice, and humanity of Western civilization. All these topics and many more are issues that require resolution and not stalemate.

The trouble comes from the manner in which the issues are being fought. James Hunter, a leading analyst of the culture wars, describes the net effect as "a public discourse defined by the art and trade of negation."[4] Name-calling, insult, ridicule, guilt by association, caricature, innuendo, accusation, denunciation, negative ads, and deceptive and manipulative videos have replaced deliberation and debate. Neither side talks *to* the other side, only *about* them; and there is no pretence of democratic engagement, let alone a serious effort at persuasion.

Needless to say, the culture-war industry is lucrative as well as politically profitable, and a swelling band of profiteering culture warriors are rushing to strike gold with their wild attacks on the other side, all for the consumption of their own supporters and the promotion of their books and programs. But the toll of such trench warfare on the republic is heavy.

First, the incessant culture warring trivializes and distorts important issues and reduces America to a Punch-and-Judy democracy in which cartoon stereotypes rail at each other with no serious engagement, let alone deliberation and debate.

Second, the culture wars demean the participants themselves. Many who start with thoughtful positions slip into a partisanship in which team playing trumps truth, decency degenerates into malice, and constant attacks become a hostility that hardens into extremism. I can only trust that the better people at least have the grace to be ashamed in private of their conduct in public.

Third, the culture wars become a vicious circle of self-fulfilling prophecy. In the bitter clash of polar views, the truths at stake are lost and each side becomes the other's double, the closest reflection of the other, the main argument for the other, and the chief fund-raiser for the other. The finger-wagging, mudslinging accusations reinforce the perceptions of the other side as the dangerous and aggressive enemy. Every conservative becomes "the Far Right," and every liberal "the Far Left." What some do once is taken to stand for all that the enemy "is really about." Each side, hypocritical enough to pretend that it lives up to its own hype, is equally insistent that the other side's worst is truly all that it is. American political advertising is sinking slowly toward a level worthy of Soviet propaganda.

And so it goes—and the unsurprising outcome is a permanent hostility that is the fulfillment of the prophecies and a savage rending of the common life.

Regrettably, the same vicious circle that bedevils the culture wars can now be seen in the rhetoric through which some people conduct the "conflict of civilizations," and especially the clash between the West and Islamism. In both cases, the issues are real and important, but the rhetoric is counterproductive. There really is a cultural divide within the United States, just as there really are tensions between civilizations in the world, but the substance of the differences is overwhelmed by the strategies of response. The vicious cycle of demonization and counterdemonization brings to bear more heat than light, and it is a far cry from an earlier generation's realism in

George Kennan's policy of containment, or from that generation's wisdom in choosing policies that consciously aim to
"do no harm."

One difference between conservatives and liberals is that
conservatives are currently unashamed of demonizing their
enemies both at home and abroad, whereas liberals tend to
criticize the demonization internationally yet indulge in it
shamelessly at home. The same people who are too sophis-
ticated to speak of an "axis of evil" or of "Islamo-fascists"
are only too happy to fire at their fellow Americans such ep-
ithets as "theocrats," "American ayatollahs," and "Christian
fascists."

Can anyone separate the snarling dogs in the culture
wars? Is it impertinent for a foreigner to suggest how? After
thirty years of visiting the United States, and twenty of living
here, I can hardly describe the mixture of sorrow and anger
with which I witness almost daily the stupidity and destruc-
tiveness of the culture warring over religion and public life—
on both sides. Do they not appreciate the legacy entrusted to
them by the founders and its uniqueness in history? Have
they never pondered the dark logic of what devastated Belfast and Beirut earlier and what devastates Baghdad now?
Do they not care enough for their descendants to look beyond the horizons of the immediate and the self-interested
and look at the long term and the common good?

No nation in history, however glorious its achievements, is
either justice incarnate or freedom fulfilled; and the United
States is no exception. But if no society ever achieves perfect
justice and perfect freedom, that means the task of criticizing
present levels of justice and freedom is never finished, and
those who love freedom and justice can never stand still. But
why then are there so few constructive solutions to the cul-

ture warring put forward? Why do so many political leaders think only of their short-term interests and wind up reinforcing the culture wars rather than trying to remedy them?

In 1988 a member of Ronald Reagan's cabinet said to me, "While I am here, I will make sure you never get to the president to speak of a civil public square, because the culture wars are in the interests of the Republicans."

"They may be today," I answered, "though tomorrow they may equally flow in the interests of the Democrats. But what matters more is that in the long run, they do not flow in the interests of America or Americans."

What is to be done? First, Americans must critically appraise the conduct of the present controversies (the focus of this chapter and the next). And second, Americans must reforge the public philosophy, and its moral and political requirements; and thus work toward a reappropriation of the constitutional heritage through citizens engaging in a new debate reordered in accord with constitutional first principles and considerations of the common good (the focus of chapter six).

The holy-war front of the culture wars has many dimensions, and they all play their part. The conflicts can be analyzed, for instance, as a clash between faiths and ideologies, as the secularists versus the fundamentalists.

Or again, it can be seen as clash between two styles of thinking and two personality types: the relativists versus the fundamentalists; the "betrayers," for whom all is gray and there are no principles of any kind that cannot be compromised at a price, and the "bitter-enders," who are intent on pressing the logic of their positions to the very end (the modern equivalent of Burke's two great menaces, "infidelity and blind zeal"[5]).

Or yet again, the conflict can be viewed in part as the unwitting product of the "mediated" age and its need for sound bites, sensationalism, verbal blood sports, and red-meat appeals to emotionalism.

Given a thirty-second time slot on television, what ratings-conscious producer would choose to have a nuanced moderate voice rather than a cockfight between stereotypical opponents? And who can read more than half a dozen direct-mail letters without realizing that the words underlined in red are all emotionally laden thrusts at the jugular of fear and hatred?

"Moderates," as it is said, "have no mailing lists." "Clean campaigns lose." "Conflict sells." "The best ads are the worst ads." "It's the mud, stupid."

But when we have sorted out all these different dimensions and given them their place, the nub of the matter is still the core conflict between *two radically opposed views of the relationship of religion and public life.* It is these views that we must examine, and it is these views with which this generation of American leaders must have the courage to break. For too long Americans have allowed the warlords of the culture wars to expand their power until they dominate many of the spheres of public life like bullies on a playground. It is time for concerned Americans to say, "A pox on both your houses!" and to reclaim the public square for citizens of all faiths.

Say No to the "Sacred Public Square"

On one side in the culture wars are the partisans of a *sacred public square,* those who for religious, historical, or cultural reasons would continue to give a preferred place in public life to one religion—which in most current cases would be the

Christian faith but one day could conceivably be the Muslim faith. Do they support an officially established national faith? No. Some, such as Christian "Reconstructionists," would like to, but they are the fringe, and the religious-liberty clauses of the First Amendment forbid it unambiguously. So on issue after issue, most argue for a preferred or privileged place for faith, if only as a vestige from the past, as in the demand for prayer in public schools today.

Most supporters of a sacred public square can be found in the ranks of the Religious Right. But then, the sharpest and most penetrating attacks on the Religious Right are because of its support for a sacred public square, or its failure to distinguish itself from that fear. And I agree wholeheartedly with this criticism. *In a society as religiously diverse as America today, for the state or federal government to continue to give any one faith a preferred or privileged position is neither just nor workable.*

To be fair, the Religious Right has been much maligned. Since it emerged as a force on the political scene in the mid-1970s, fundamentalism has become the "eighth deadly sin," and we have seen one long open season on fundamentalism and those who have been variously insulted as "American ayatollahs," "theocrats," "Christianists," "theocons," and now "Christian fascists." There is good reason for the updated version of Peter Vierek's comment that antifundamentalism has replaced anti-Catholicism as the anti-Semitism of the intellectual.

Kevin Phillips, for example, has recently appeared on countless radio and television shows warning darkly of an "American theocracy." But his is only the latest in a series of fevered liberal alarms that include fictional works, such as Margaret Atwood's *The Handmaid's Tale,* and nonfiction works whose warnings of what conservative Christians will require when they have their way in America are frankly ludicrous and unworthy of fair-minded liberals and serious reporters.

Polls confirm that the decision to be "progressive" or "traditionalist" not only predetermines but precedes political choices. Liberals, in other words, choose to be progressive before they choose their policies, and are often no more independent in their thinking than traditionalists. But those who still prize fair-mindedness might consider the following:

First, there is little in the traditionalist platform that would not have been the concerns of most Americans as recently as the 1950s.

Second, if such concerns qualify as "theocracy" and "Christian fascism," many of America's most revered leaders in most earlier periods in American history would have been theocrats and fascists, too.

Third, ruling out today's movements as "theocratic" because of the influence of religion would also rule out such shining successful reforms as the abolition of slavery and the civil rights movement, both of which—like almost all Western reform movements—were inspired by faith and led by people of faith.

Fourth, progressives who make such wild, inaccurate, and ill-tempered attacks end by becoming like those they attack, and their works take their place as astonishing exhibits of what otherwise decent people may think under the alarmist conditions of the culture wars.

The root trouble is that Phillips, and all the antitheocrats, define *theocracy* so loosely—for Phillips, it is "some degree of rule by religion"—that it would include (and therefore exclude) any influence of faith on public life.[6] Some already use *theocracy* as the term of choice by which to object to every trace of faith in public life, as if the slightest public mention of God were enough to rekindle the fires of the Inquisition, and the merest whisper of a prayer were dangerous enough to warrant calling out the separationist police and their legal henchmen.

When the merest *influence* of a faith or philosophy on life is taken as tantamount to *rule by religion* and therefore as *theocracy,* the outcome is a disbarring of both Madison's "free exercise" of faith and Socrates' "examined life." For "free exercise" could always be confused with "undue influence of religion," and such a definition of theocracy would block any thoughtful person from seeking to lead an intelligent life with integrity—liberals no less than fundamentalists, and atheists, Jews, Buddhists, and Mormons as much as Christians and Muslims. For which of us who prize the high place of reason and integrity would not desire to lead a life influenced and "ruled" by whatever we believe is true, right, good, and beautiful—and to persuade others of the merits of doing so, too?

Common sense, not to speak of history and a sense of humor, could save America from much of the absurdity of its current rhetoric. The difference between *free exercise* and *theocracy* is simple, clear, and telling, yet in the fevered climate of the culture wars the two are taken as one. To paraphrase H. L. Mencken, today's puritan is the person who is haunted by the thought that someone somewhere may possibly have breathed up a prayer in the public square.

Similarly, when Phillips proves the dangers of "the emerging Republican theocracy"—as he does by showing the numerical and political strength of the Southern Baptist Convention—he flies in the face of any fair-minded view of history. I am not a Baptist, but to accuse the heirs of Roger

Williams, John Leland, and Isaac Backus of theocracy would be greeted as a trifle exaggerated, if not absurd, were it not for reviewers and readers ready to cheer for any attack on people they dislike.

Their Own Worst Enemies

All that said, there is no question that the Religious Right deserves much of the dismissal and dislike it has brought down on its own head. If the follies, blunders, misdemeanors, and gaffes of its leaders had not been committed, they would be hard to invent.

As one who holds the Hebrew prophets in the highest esteem, I am outraged by the false prophets of fundamentalism, who violate the biblical canons of prophecy and pronounce in the name of the Lord what is theologically obscene and historically untrue.

As one who is challenged to the core by the sublime call of Jesus of Nazareth that his followers should "love your enemies, do good to those who hate you, bless those who curse you, and pray for those who abuse you,"[7] I am appalled by the way the Religious Right attacks its fellow believers and demonizes its enemies. Shame on the scurrilous attacks in much Christian direct mail, and on fundamentalist pastors and their followers who hold placards in public such as "God hates fags," "Thank God for maimed soldiers," and "God hates you."

They claim to speak for Christ and for Christians, but their culture warring is closer to Karl Kraus's satire, in his essay "The Last Days of Mankind," of a Protestant minister who assures his congregation that Jesus' command is restricted to individuals and does not apply to political parties or nations: "In the struggle of the nations, there is no room for loving one's enemies. Here the individual soldier need have no scruples! In the heat of battle Jesus' command of love is suspended!"[8]

Against all such hypocrisies, Wendell Berry rightly protests: "The Christian gospel is a summons to peace, calling for justice beyond anger, mercy beyond justice, and love beyond forgiveness."[9]

As one who believes that the call of Jesus is to a path of suffering that shuts the door to every form of victim-playing, I am angered by organizers of the Religious Right who play the victim card and appeal openly to Christian resentment. Recently, senators and representatives addressed a conference in Washington, D.C., called "The War on Christians," with book titles and topics such as "The Criminalization of Christianity." "Of course, there is a war on Christianity," the former Republican majority leader in the House declared to a rousing ovation. "You guys are the Jews of the twenty-first century," a Jewish activist and sympathizer said.[10]

Do they not know that those who portray themselves as victims come to perceive themselves as victims and then to paralyze themselves as victims? In the late 1980s, when the Moral Majority was faltering, certain leaders of the Religious Right deliberately passed around the slogan that Christians were a "small persecuted minority," victimized by the liberal elites—and did so just as other activist groups were giving up the rhetoric of the victim card.

But whether "victimization" then or a "war on Christians" now, such tactics of the Religious Right are foolish, ineffectual, and downright anti-Christian. The problem is not that these people are theocrats, but that they are sub-Christian. They do not violate the separation of church and state so much as they violate Christian integrity. Factually, it is dead wrong for Christians to portray themselves as a minority, let alone as persecuted. Christians are as close to a majority community as any group in America; what their fellow Christians are facing today in China, North Korea, Burma, and Sudan is real persecution.

Psychologically, victim-playing is dangerous because it represents what Nietzsche called "the politics of the tarantula," a base appeal to resentment. But worst of all, it is spiritually hypocritical, for nothing so contradicts their claim to represent "Christian values" as their refusal to follow the teaching and example of Jesus of Nazareth by playing the victim card and finding an excuse not to love their enemies. Shame, shame, shame on such people; and woe, woe, woe to such tactics.

To go deeper and to put the point bluntly: as these few examples show, *many in the Religious Right are more obviously fundamentalists than they are Christians.* By that I do not mean that they are not Christians, but that the overlay of their fundamentalism has so overpowered their Christian faith that the substance and style of their political action have little to do with Jesus. They have lost their Christian core and become a political movement that at times has little discernible Christian remainder.

There are three main traditions in the Christian faith that trace themselves all the way back to Jesus himself—the Orthodox, the Roman Catholic, and the Evangelical. But fundamentalism is not traditional. Its origins were in an early-twentieth-century Christian movement that responded to the rise of theological liberalism with "a concern for the fundamentals" of faith, a concern for fundamentals that no self-respecting sports coach could quarrel with. But fundamentalism has long since morphed beyond these worthy origins, and today it has become a worldwide phenomenon that touches all the world's religions, and even secularism, too.

As such, fundamentalism is not traditional; it is an essentially modern reaction to the modern world. While it has a religious identity, it is as much a social movement. What it does is reassert a lost world, a once-intact but no longer taken-for-granted cultural reality; and in doing so, it both romanticizes the past, with its messiness airbrushed away, and radicalizes the present with its overlay of psychological defiance and cultural militancy. In the process, Christian fundamentalism grows more and more alien to the way of life to which Jesus of Nazareth called his followers.

This point about Christian fundamentalism being a modern reaction to the modern world carries a double warning about the perils of extremism—and the fact that "my enemy's enemies" are not always my friends. On the one hand, such a reaction to the modern world has betrayed the church in the past. The German Christians who fell for the siren sounds of Nazism were the very ones who had set out to fight for "the order of God as the standard for the shaping of common life" (in the words of a Protestant theologian), over against the forces of corrupt individualism and liberalism, represented by the Weimar age and its permissiveness, abortions, decadence, and dismissal of traditional marriage.[11]

With such an impulse, it was all too easy for Hitler to corral their support in coming to power. "The national government will regard its first and foremost duty," he declared, "to restore the unity and spirit of our People. It will preserve and defend the foundations upon which the power of our nation rests. It will take Christianity, as the basis of our collective morality, and the family as the nucleus of our People and State, under its firm protection."[12]

On the other hand, the same extreme reaction to the modern world can be seen in other religions, such as Islamic fundamentalism. If the lost world of the American Religious Right lies in the nineteenth century, the lost world of Islamists is the seventh century, when Muhammad and his followers swept everything before them. *Salafism,* the word used of Muslim fundamentalists, literally means a "harking back." But Islamism is far more than just a throwback to primitive or medieval Islam. Its view of its advocates as a revolutionary vanguard, and their belief in the power of violence to remake humanity, are highly modern ideas and closer to the views of nineteenth-century anarchists and nihilists than to those of their Muslim forebears. As such, Islamism is truly a modern reaction to the modern world.

In the same way, the Religious Right's references to its enemies and its use of tactics such as direct mail, talk radio, and victim playing owe more to fundamentalist reactions to modernity and to overheated fictional visions of the end times than to the good news of Jesus of Nazareth. As an observer quipped of the "Left Behind" craze, which has intoxicated and diverted so many fundamentalists and become conflated in the public mind with the Christian view, "For God so loved the world that he gave us World War Three."

In short, many of the tactics of the Religious Right serve only to illustrate the cynics' quip "The Christian Right is neither," and to underscore the sad wisdom of Erasmus, who witnessed the insanities of Christians in his day: "If we would bring the Turks to Christianity, we must first be Christians."

Let me be plain. In writing critically of fundamentalism and the Religious Right, I do not write as a skeptic toward faith or as a supporter of the strict separationist view that would confine faith to the private sphere. I write as a Christian who takes my own faith seriously with all the integrity of classical, historic orthodoxy, just as I respect the right and duty of others to take their faith seriously, too, whether religious or naturalistic. But when all is said and done, I have two further objections to the Religious Right.

Word Above Sword and Ballot Box

First, the Religious Right has politicized faith, a cardinal error that is wrong in both principle and practice—again, not as a constitutional matter but as a matter of Christian integrity that has political consequences. Historically, evangelicals have a distinguished record in politics, exemplified by their broad contributions to liberal reforms and by leading individuals such as William Wilberforce, "the little liberator" who, among many historic reforms, led the abolition of slavery throughout the British Empire and stands as the greatest social reformer in all history.

Fundamentalism, by contrast, was originally inward-looking in faith and inactive in politics. It was disinterested in politics just as it was generally world-denying in its cultural stance—exemplified famously by Jerry Falwell's 1965 sermon in which he contrasted "ministers and marchers" and called his hearers to "preach the Word" but not to "reform the externals." Fundamentalism's recent engagement with politics, especially after the late 1970s, is therefore uncharacteristic.

But Christians, who should be engaged in politics, should never be equated without remainder with any political party or ideology, or fall for the fallacy of "particularism"—the idea that there is a single, particular party or policy that is uniquely and fully Christian. There are parties and policies that are *not* Christian, but there is no one party or set of policies that uniquely is. The City of God coincides but is never conflated with the City of Man, and the people of God can never be identified exclusively with any state or party.

This means that, for Christians, there is a vital difference between proper political engagement and the danger of politicization—the subservience of the Christian faith to the political agendas and political styles of its day, so that faith loses its integrity and independence and becomes the reflection of politics.

This objection to politicization may sound like a domestic quarrel for Christians. At one level it is, though I include it here because its practical outcome affects citizens of all faiths. As the heirs of the Jewish tradition, Christians have a distinctive view of power, expressed in the maxim "Word above sword." Whereas Israel's neighboring nations viewed their warrior-king as their chief political officer, the Jews held that God was their warrior-king; and in an early and distinctive expression of the separation of "church and state," they held that God had several political officers apart from the king, such as the priest and the prophet. (According to the Hebrew record, God did not originally even intend Israel to have a king.) Of these other officers, the enduring, indispensable, and decisive one was the prophet, whose role in national crises proved more crucial to the Jews than that of the kings and the priests.

Thus the prophet—who was the messenger of God, with no power base but the word of God—was more important to the people of God than the king, whose power base was the sword. Indeed, while the Hebrew prophets took on many causes, their main thrust was directed against the royal nationalism that distorted Jewish life, just as presidential nationalism distorts American life today.

Unquestionably, Jesus of Nazareth understood himself as standing in the same prophetic tradition, relying decisively on the Word and repudiating the party of the Zealots and all who rely primarily on the sword. ("Those who take to the sword shall die by the sword.") It was therefore a disastrous detour when the Christian church allowed the Emperor Constantine to reach for the mantle of her moral authority to cover the state. ("What I will," his son Constantius announced, "should be the law of the church,"[13] a sentiment later echoed by Louis XIV: "*L'Eglise, c'est moi.*") Or when the Renaissance popes reached for the sword of the princely states to enhance the power of the church. Or when the Protestant church in Germany submitted weakly to the Nazi Party in the 1930s and allowed itself to be used as a support. (Hitler: "We can make this clerical gang go the way we want, quite easily."[14])

Each of these gross errors was different, though all three stemmed from false ways of engaging public life. But whatever the different motives, the Christian church in Europe has yet to escape from the long, dark shadow of this seventeen-hundred-year dangerous liaison of church and state.

In America, the brilliant separation of church and state freed the churches from the deadly clutches of this embrace. If the churches were to have influence, it had to be first and foremost through a reliance on the Word rather than the sword or the ballot box, and it was better to come through laypeople rather than pastors or priests, and to be indirect and "bottom up" rather than direct and "top down."

Thus when Tocqueville came to the United States in 1831, he found it striking that religion was "the first of the political institutions"—even though pastors "keep aloof from politics" and though "faith takes no direct part in the government of society."[15] In other words, the influence of the church was all the stronger for being indirect and that of the pastors all the stronger for their being at one remove from political engagement. Politics in all its gritty realism is the proper calling of lay people, not the prime business of the pulpit. Christians should be engaged in politics, but never equated without remainder with any party or ideology.

Put differently, there are two equal but opposite errors into which Christians have fallen in the modern world. One error is to "privatize" faith, interpreting and applying it to the personal and spiritual realm only. That way faith loses its *integrity* and becomes "privately engaging and publicly irrelevant."

The other error, represented by the Religious Left in the 1960s and the Religious Right since the late 1970s, is to "politicize" faith, using faith to express essentially political points that have lost touch with biblical truth. That way faith loses its *independence*, the church becomes "the regime at prayer," Christians become the "useful idiots" or "biddable foot soldiers" for one political party or another, and the Christian faith becomes an ideology in its purest form: Christian beliefs are used as weapons for political interests. In short, out of anxiety about a vanishing culture or in a foolish exchange for an illusory promise of power, Christians are cheated into bartering away their identity, motives, language, passions, and votes.

Kevin Phillips delivers his scathing attack on "radicalized religion" in a chapter titled "Too Many Preachers." But the problem is not too many preachers; proportionately, there are no more than before. The problem is too many preachers in the wrong place with the wrong text and the wrong tone. Preachers should be in the pulpit preaching the Word, including its relevance to politics and to the whole of life, but leaving their laypeople to be in the public square and to apply their faith to politics.

Faith's loss of independence through politicization is more damaging than it might appear, for the cultural captivity of the Christian Right represents a double loss of independence. Rather obviously, Christians lose their independence when they engage in politics in a way that allows their faith to become subservient to politics and its priorities and procedures. But less obvious and equally important, Christians have already lost their independence when they attempt to find political solutions for problems that are essentially cultural and prepolitical—in other words, when they ask politics to do what politics cannot do.

When there has been a profound sea change in culture, as the United States has experienced since the 1960s, it is both foolish and futile to think that it can be reversed and restored by politics alone. That approach will always fail, and can only fail. Politics is downstream from the deep and important changes in American culture, and what lies upstream is mostly beyond the reach of political action. Thus overreaching political activism is bound not only to fail, but to leave the cultural changes more deeply entrenched than ever and those fighting them weaker than ever.

James Davison Hunter nails the point sharply: "Cultural conservatives bet on politics as the means to respond to the changes in the world, but that politics can only be a losing strategy. What political solution is there to the absence of decency? To the spread of vulgarity? To the lack of civility and the want of compassion? The answer, of course, is none— there are no political solutions to these concerns, and the headlong pursuit of them by conservatives will lead, inevitably, to failure."[16]

Christians from both sides of the political spectrum, Left as well as Right, have made the same mistake of politicizing faith; and signs are that a weakening of the Religious Right will lead to a rejuvenation of the Religious Left, which would be no better. And it must be remembered that the present alliance between Christian conservatives and the GOP was in part a defensive reaction to the decision of the Democratic Party in 1972 to shift from its traditional alliances and espouse the cause of secularism. But whichever side it comes from, politicized preaching is faithless, foolish, and disastrous for the church—and disastrous first and foremost for Christian reasons rather than constitutional reasons.

The Christian Right should be under no illusions. Its recent politicization of faith is an expression of folly, not wisdom, and a sign of its weakness, not strength. As Father Richard John Neuhaus tirelessly reminds Christians engaging with public life, "The first thing to say about politics is that politics is not the first thing."[17]

Justice or Just Us?

Second, the Religious Right has consistently exhibited one glaring weakness that is proving its Achilles' heel and will lead to its final undoing. It has never articulated a clear public philosophy, or a common vision for the public good. It has never set out its own claims within a framework of what is just and free for everyone else, too. As a result, every claim the Religious Right makes and every thrust it exerts into the public sphere appear to those who fear it, or oppose it as "theocratic" and "coercive," an undue "imposition" of one set of values over the values of others in a pluralistic society. As a journalist remarked to me in the 1980s, "The Religious Right talks of justice, but sounds like 'just us.'"

There are many roots to this deficiency—ranging from a failure to apply the Golden Rule of Jesus, to a distorted understanding of history, to an inability to make persuasive and accessible arguments in the public square. But the net result is disastrous. The Religious Right has become the best argument for its worst opponents, the most powerful factor in its own rejection, and a prime reason for the repudiation of religion in contemporary America.

For the American republic, the last of these three points is the most crucial. Those who appreciate the founders' position on the importance of faiths for sustainable freedom must not fail to learn the lessons of European experience. Relate church and state wrongly, and the result is lethal for both. But a mere reaction to the wrong relationship, understandable though it is, is no better; and the resulting settlement may well prove deficient for the future of European civilization. Those who strangled the last king with the guts of the last priest may have fatally shortened the life of democracy, too.

As we have seen, the separation of church and state is America's wisest and most brilliant solution to the problem of religion and public life, and so European-style reactions have never been America's problem. With Tocqueville's "spirit of liberty" and the "spirit of religion" walking hand in hand, the United States has never had significant hostility between particular faiths or significant antipathy toward faith itself—until recently. Religious liberty and diversity have complemented rather than contradicted each other, with religious liberty making diversity more likely and diversity making religious liberty more necessary.

Let there be no misunderstanding. This situation is now changing. Americans cannot rely on the earlier American settlement as if it were part of the American genes and will last forever. With the rise of the culture wars in the last generation, with the extremes on both sides, and with the persistent failure of the Religious Right to address the issue of the common vision for the common good, the earlier settlement has broken down, and the landscape is beginning to change in a way that has incalculable consequences for the future.

There is a dangerous roadside bomb on the path down which the Religious Right is driving recklessly. Reinforced by its lack of a public philosophy as well as by its near-iron-clad links with the Republican Party, the electoral power and the apocalyptic style of the Religious Right are generating the greatest backlash against the Christian faith in American history, especially among educated people—and will continue to do so unless wiser voices and a more generous vision prevail. Tocqueville's spirit of religion and spirit of liberty are beginning to march in a French direction.

Ironically, this equation of the Religious Right with Republicanism and nationalism is happening at the very time when many of the European churches are going in the opposite direction. Waking up to the lessons of history, they are severing their disastrous links with the structures of power and becoming independent Christian voices and actors, engaging public life on a wide range of issues, from human rights and stewardship of the earth to the concerns of civil society.

Evangelicals are the ones most affected by the mounting backlash against the Religious Right, for they are the ones now identified with all the follies of fundamentalism and the extremism of the Religious Right. But evangelicals are not fundamentalists. Jerry Falwell liked to say that "fundamentalists are evangelicals with guts." But any mite of truth in his remark is offset by a mountain of a problem: fundamentalism and the Religious Right now represent the greatest single barrier to Americans appreciating the "good news" that defines what it is to be evangelical and Christian.

The vehemence and viciousness of the attacks on the Christian faith are rising, and the membership of atheist groups (though not the number of atheists) is growing—all as a direct response to the Religious Right. The overall message should be as clear to evangelicals as it is to atheists: "If the Christian Right is what religion means, then more and more educated people do not want to be religious."

Will Christians wake up from their slumber and shake off this political and cultural baggage that is undoing them? Will evangelicals reaffirm their real identity, reform their corrupt behavior, and reposition themselves in public life in clear contrast to fundamentalism and the Religious Right? Will they recover an independent voice in public life that is constructive and more expressive of a full range of Christian concerns?

It should be far easier for evangelicals to renounce the privileges and powers of their nineteenth-century Protestant dominance than it was for Catholics to renounce their far older and far more powerful established status in Europe and elsewhere. But the Roman Catholic Church has done exactly that. In little more than one generation it has shifted from being the last bastion of the ancien régime to being in the vanguard of the movement for worldwide justice and human rights.

The choice for American evangelicals is blunt. As followers of one who put aside the power and status that was his by right, and emptied himself to become a servant, the principle should be the only argument needed, though the pragmatic incentive is plain. It would be bad enough if evangelicals were to pursue power and gain the world at the risk of losing their souls. But it would be stupid beyond belief to pursue power and gain virtually nothing—in other words, to sell their birthright for a mess of political pottage.

There is more to the pragmatic urgency. Unless evangelicals achieve such a reaffirmation, reformation, and repositioning, the continuing confusion with fundamentalism and the Religious Right will produce the very outcome that they fear. We are already seeing the rise of a European-style reaction to religion in the public square. If it hardens, it will change America for generations and maybe forever; and evangelicals will have no one to blame but themselves.

Chapter Five

Say No to the
Naked Public Square

"Most Christians would sooner die than think—in fact they do." In my mind's eye I can still hear Bertrand Russell delivering that favorite line of his with a deadpan face, betrayed only by the twinkle in his eye. It was the early 1960s, I was a student and living in London, and the air was electric with the passions and debates of the rising counterculture. Russell, by contrast, was in his nineties, fighting nuclear weapons with unabated vigor, and his craggy, aquiline face was the perfect profile for the secular prophet he was. As his quip shows, he was more than willing to take sideswipes at any with whom he disagreed, but it was usually with grace and often with humor.

Years later as a graduate student at Oxford, I shared a train compartment with the eminent philosopher A. J. Ayer—or Professor Sir Alfred J. Ayer, as he had become. My field was the social sciences, but I had read a fair amount of philosophy, and I certainly knew the fate of Ayer's logical positivism and his celebrated "verification principle." Only that which could be tested by the five senses, he had argued, could be verified as true. Theology was therefore "nonsense"; or, as it was famously argued, "The word G-O-D is less meaningful than the word D-O-G." His was the ironclad atheism of a world without windows.

The trouble for A. J. Ayer was that his verification principle was self-refuting. It could not verify itself and thus opened itself up to the charge of being nonsense, too. As he admitted, what he thought was a guillotine against faith turned out to be a "blind alley." He was candid with me about the failure of his principle. "I wish I had been more consistent," he chuckled. "Any iconoclast who brandishes a debunker's sword should be required to demonstrate it publicly on his own cherished beliefs."

It is true that Lord Russell was an aristocrat and that A. J. Ayer had been knighted and was retired when I spoke to him. But in countless other cases in those days, there was a civility to atheist arguments that matched the force of their logic and rigor. Anyone who reads Russell's "A Free Man's Worship" can still enjoy the pathos and beauty that offsets the bleak bravery of its vision of a world leading from "accidental collocations of atoms" to "extinction in the vast death of the solar system."[1] And Ayer was usually as polite as he was formidable in his decisive dismissals of beliefs with which he disagreed.

I have known many secularists over the years, many of them as dedicated as Russell and Ayer, though not so well known. I have also read the books of many others, both those living and those who no longer grace the earth. But to put it charitably, when I read the current dismissals of faith from the new atheists published in America today, I do not get the impression of the same calm assurance, strenuous logic, and passion for truth. We are closer to the wild atheism of Madalyn Murray O'Hair, back to barnyard debating, with ungrounded assertions, irresponsible accusations, ad hominem arguments, and reasoning that repeatedly slumps into ranting.

It appears that the temperature is mounting. In the six weeks after the election of George W. Bush in 2004, the press and airwaves were thick with the vented anger of disappointed liberals and secularists whose dire alarms were as apocalyptic as the wildest pages of the "Left Behind" novels. Many accusations are as overheated as they are ludicrous—for example, the claims mentioned in chapter one that Christians are as dangerous as Muslim extremists, or that fundamentalists are as bad as Ku Klux Klansmen. Which would such accusers like to have following them down the street to their home on a dark evening—an al Qaeda jihadist wearing a suicide belt or a Focus on the Family radio listener carrying a Bible?

Doubtless there will be detailed replies to arguments such as Richard Dawkins's *The God Delusion*, Sam Harris's bestselling *The End of Faith* and his *Letter to a Christian Nation*. In fact there already have been, though astonishingly Dawkins and Harris brush off reasoned replies and keep on as if some of their arguments had not been decisively refuted.[2] But beyond the strengths and weaknesses of the specific arguments, there are two deep deficiencies in the secularist outburst that bear on the present discussion.

For a start, they write out of a frustration that betrays the irrationality of what they declare is their fight for reason. Dawkins joins John Lennon in imagining a world without religion, and hopes for his book that "religious readers who open it will be atheists when they put it down."[3] He also says he hopes to drive religion not only from the public square but from society altogether. Harris, as his title indicates, has as his object "the end of faith," and claims that "the days of our religious identities are clearly numbered."[4] Yet he also acknowledges that his second book "is the product of failure—the failure of the many attacks on religion that preceded it, the failure of our schools to announce the death of God in a way that each generation can understand."[5]

Do Dawkins, Harris, and their ilk really hope to succeed in consigning faith to the dustbin of history? Do they really believe that religion will disappear under the scrutiny of their arguments? What philosophical, anthropological, and historical reasons do they give for their trust in the end of faith and the triumph of their narrow secular reason? When has such reason ever been able to justify itself without toppling into skepticism and irrationality, as we have seen once more with postmodernism? Where has secularism ever appealed widely to most ordinary people when it has not been imposed by coercion, as under the communists?

For all its strength in certain educated circles, the secularist worldview is simply too bleak and too bloodless for most ordinary people. (As one atheist leader admits, atheists are predominant among the "upper 5 percent. Where we're lagging is among the lower 95 percent."[6]) Even at the higher level, many of the greatest philosophers and scientists today are not only unconvinced by the atheist arguments, but give equally powerful arguments for the rationality of their faith in God.

Writing as a thoughtful Christian (and, like Dawkins, a graduate of Oxford with an advanced degree), I take seriously the ideal of the "examined life" and repudiate completely his description of all religious believers as unquestioning "faith-heads" who believe on unreasoning and unwarranted "blind trust." I therefore find it curious to be treated by Muslims as a second-class citizen and by atheists as a second-class thinker—a *dhimmi* to one and a dummy to the other.

But what matters goes beyond the personal. Are the new atheists in fact rational and right to believe in the end of faith? From everything I know and have ever read about humanity and the deepest human thinking about religion, Dawkins's and Harris's faith in the end of faith is irrational, incredible, and fantastic, though in some ways deeply touching. By all means join John Lennon and "imagine a world without religion"—"Let it be," as the famous four sang elsewhere—but have the candor and humility to admit that such a world is entirely imaginary, and likely to remain so. Like all utopias, the atheist utopia is literally "no place," and when real atheists have tried to inaugurate it in the real world, their efforts have been murderous beyond belief, as my boyhood in China never allows me to forget.

No leap of faith by the most anti-intellectual of religious believers could be more blindly trusting and irrational than that of these self-professed devotees of reason. If they are to sustain their faith in reason, and at the same time prevent it from becoming a religion of Reason that will once again be a spawning ground for terror as secular reason has so often been since the eighteenth century, they will find that they need faith as both a basis and a boundary for their reason. At the end of the day, reason generates faith just as faith guarantees reason. We understand in order to believe, and we believe in order to understand.

That is a discussion for another time. What matters here is that, for better or worse, the vast accumulated evidence of the human story would suggest that religion will persist as long as human beings are still around. For someone who declares himself so committed to reason to be so irrational means that Harris's frustration can only mount. He is either in for a rethink or in for even more frustration.

It is tempting to wonder whether there is a link between the rise in secularist ire and the collapse of secularization theory. *Secularism*, the philosophy, could afford to stand back and watch when *secularization*, the process, was said to be sweeping everything before it. There was no need for the atheist's helpful shove when religion was about to disappear anyway. But regardless of explanations, what is beyond doubt is that secularist anger has risen in America in direct reaction to the perceived extremes and dangers of the Religious Right, with Islamic extremism behind them.

Simone de Beauvoir, Jean-Paul Sartre's lifelong companion, showed an atheism with a humbler face. When asked by a journalist what she felt about creating a body of work that negated the existence of God, she replied wryly, "One can abolish water, but one cannot abolish thirst."

Double Intolerance

Such irrationality is only the start of the problem. Arguments such as Dawkins's and Harris's are also openly and brazenly intolerant. In fact, these men pride themselves on their double intolerance: they are intolerant not only of those they consider religious extremists, they are also of religious moderates, whom they consider enablers of the extremists. In short, they are intolerant of all religion. "We can no longer afford the luxury of such political correctness," Harris writes about religious moderates. "We can no more tolerate a diversity of religious beliefs than a diversity of beliefs about epidemiology and basic hygiene."[7]

Such brazen and irresponsible intolerance, based on a cavalier ignorance of the principles and history of religious liberty, is understandable from Dawkins, the European, but harder to imagine from an American, as Harris is. Equally, it is shameful that their intolerance has been applauded by many liberals who turn a blind eye to any attack on those they consider extremists. But we must not overlook a damaging consequence of this new and open intolerance. The United States is beginning to see increasingly vicious arguments against other faiths and their truthfulness in the public square.

Such arguments between faiths are legitimate and urgent, but they should be made, and answered, only with great care. There is a broad overlap, with no exact boundaries, between the public square and public life. But we should be clear that it is playing with fire to begin to argue in the public square about whether different faiths are true—because of the very seriousness of truth. Nothing is more precious and potent than truth, but nothing is more dangerous than to debate such arguments in the public square. Before long the different sides will go for the jugular, and verbal violence will issue in conflicts that are as ugly as they are insoluble. As Erasmus warned many centuries ago, the danger is that the long war of words and writings will end in blows.

Please do not misunderstand my point. I am not arguing that faith should be "privileged," as if it required kid-gloves discussion for fear of causing offense and of setting off politically correct protests among the hypersensitive victimized or riots in other parts of the world. Truth and tough-minded debates about truth are the oxygen of a free society. So if any beliefs, held by any citizens, are thought by any others to be irrational and a delusion, they should be addressed trenchantly and fearlessly. The politics of "no offense" is a recipe for cowardice and appeasement. Atheists have every right to speak out, to argue for, and to attack whatever they choose. The question for them is whether their arguments are good arguments, or whether they will suffer the fate of most of their predecessors before them.

What is more, followers of Jesus are not offended by attacks, and at this point Christians part company with followers of the prophet Muhammad. The sort of attacks that Muslims take as an insult to the Prophet are what Christians see as central to the mission of Jesus. The symbol that is literally the crux of the Christian faith is not a fashion accessory but an instrument of torture and execution for criminals, and on it is one who was spread-eagled naked at the moment of his most excruciating pain and abandonment.

Yet such insult, humiliation, torture, disfigurement, and death were at the heart of what Jesus came to do, and knew that he came to do. Far from complaining about a "dire insult" or a "blasphemy" to be avenged with a fatwa or a riot or a lawsuit, Christians should see any continuing prejudice or malice toward Jesus and his followers as something to be embraced as an undeserved honor rather than protested as unfair victimization.

That said, in wise societies where the link between freedom and civility is respected, the public square is not the wisest place to examine the truth claims of different faiths. Certainly it can and should be done in the private sphere with no holds barred, and certainly, too, in public life, if done with greater care. But the public square is the place where the *roots* of faith are generally best left unspoken, and what is discussed are the *results* of faith—their implications for public policy and the common life of all citizens.

In short, my opening answer to Richard Dawkins, Sam Harris, and other secularists is to call for civility first—to establish a civil public square, within which we may all learn to respect our deepest differences and discuss them robustly but civilly and peacefully—and then in the appropriate setting, human being to human being, to explore the reasons for why we believe and all that it means. At the very least, vicious attacks on each other's faiths in the public square will aggravate the culture wars further. More serious, a climate of repeated assaults will raise the specter of the violence becoming more than verbal.

Such a call for the total eradication of religion, not only from public life but from life altogether, is unprecedented in American history, and its success unproven. Early attempts to implement it in a Communist form were murderous, to put it mildly, and current proponents must show that their purportedly liberal versions of the "end of faith" are less utopian and likely to have a constructive result. At the very least, such total secularist antagonism toward faith creates the situation today in which the great divide is not between religions but between those who take faith seriously and those who exclude it altogether. Were it not for the smugness born of the education gap between most liberals and most fundamentalists, the starkness and the significance of this chasm would be taken more seriously.

Legal Secularism

The plain fact is that certain liberals and secularists are just as responsible for the incivility of the culture wars as the Religious Right, and they form the opposing extreme. For on the other side of the culture wars from *the sacred public square* are the partisans of what Richard John Neuhaus aptly called *the naked public square*[8] (or, in Europe, is called *the empty public square*)—those who wish to make all religious expression inviolably private and to make the public sphere inviolably secular. If a vision of a sacred public square is represented broadly by the Religious Right, also known as the "reimposers" (those who would like to impose their version of an earlier state of things on everyone else), then the vision of a naked public square is represented by a diverse group of secularists, liberals, and religious believers united by their advocacy of a strict interpretation of the separation between church and state, and also known as the "removers" (those who would remove every trace of religion from public life).

Advocates of the naked public square certainly include a significant number of religious believers; there were a particularly high number of Baptists in the early days. But it is shaped by the convergence of three fundamentally secular trends: the philosophy of secularism, the political philosophy of liberalism in its late-twentieth-century form associated with John Rawls and Jürgen Habermas, and the constitutional theory of strict separation associated with Leo Pfeffer and Justice Hugo Black. This combination is so common that the position has been called "legal secularism" (or, in Europe, "programmatic secularism"), and each strand has been used to advance the others.[9] For many liberals, legal secularism is so natural and self-evident that it is their unexamined default position, so much so that any challenge to it comes as a surprise and a shock.

I argued that in a society as pluralistic as ours, a vision of a sacred public square is unjust and unworkable. The same is even more true of the naked public square. The great majority of Americans are adherents of one faith or another, so by rigorously excluding all religious expressions from public life, legal secularists severely curtail the free exercise of faith and, whether wittingly or unwittingly, give a preference and privilege to the philosophy of secularism—hence the aptness of the term "legal secularism."

Irony of Ironies

Beyond this fundamental problem, there are seven important objections to the naked public square that fair-minded liberals should consider:

First, legal secularism is unhistorical. As we saw in a previous chapter, Jefferson, who is claimed as the apostle of strict separation, did not practice separation in a manner that is anything like the demands of his followers today. If Jefferson's famous serpentine walls are straight, then his views of the separation of church and state were strict. But only a drunk could see the walls as straight, and it is hard to think that some of his followers today are really serious about history—except that, having made their case for strict separation on the grounds of history and the 1802 letter to the Danbury Baptists, they then kick away the ladder by which they climbed to their position and turn a blind eye to history.

Where then is the pursuit of truth and the intellectual honesty that Jefferson so much admired? G. K. Chesterton described the madman as the person who, far from losing his reason, has lost everything *except his reason.* In the same way, it is curious how many supporters of strict separation cite Jefferson and pride themselves on their historical foundations when the one argument they lack is history, and when Jefferson's own practices would encourage them to moderate their claims.

Second, legal secularists are philosophically inconsistent in that their worldview is only one faith among many. Secular liberals often put forward two arguments in explaining their position: that secularism is not a faith like other faiths, and that liberalism should be privileged as the coming single faith of enlightened humanity. But these two arguments are contradictory, and the assumptions behind them are pure fictions, founded on wishful thinking rather than reason or science. On the one hand, secularists are far from irreligious and "unbelievers." Secularism is a faith like any other, albeit naturalistic rather than supernatural. And on the other hand, liberalism has no rational grounds for laying claim to being the faith of humanity in the future.

Thus, to the degree that strict separationism succeeds on the basis of these fictions, secular liberals have to own up to their own deception, witting or unwitting. According to non-humanistic secularists such as the philosopher John Gray, secular humanists repress religion and religious experience in much the same way that Victorians repressed sex. But their liberalism is in fact religious, in both substance and style. Its view of human uniqueness is borrowed from the Jewish and Christian faiths, and often its style shares the same character as the creed of the *philosophes,* whom Gibbon excoriated because they preached the tenets of atheism with the bigotry of dogmatists.

Dogmatic Enlightenment bigots? Liberals should face the fact of secularist fundamentalism in their own ranks, and the uncomfortable fact that secularists are often, in the sociologist Rodney Stark's description, "the worst current offenders of norms of civility."[10] Better far the candor of Thomas Paine, who begins his *Age of Reason* with an unambiguous declaration: "I believe in one God, and no more ... my own mind is my own church."[11] Unless liberals acknowledge that their faith is one among many, liberalism will remain "the unthinking creed of thinking people."[12]

Beyond the danger of hypocrisy lies a practical injustice. When liberals insist that liberalism is not a faith, they replay the nineteenth-century privileging of Protestantism in the public schools, with liberals in the place of Protestants. Protestants in the nineteenth century were largely blind to their preferred position, which was only too obvious to minorities such as Catholics and Jews. In the same way, today's secularists who pretend they are not a faith like other faiths are indifferent to their privileged position and brush aside the objections of religious believers as inconsequential.

Bitter though it is for some secular liberals to admit, liberalism is only one way of life among others and deserves to be no more (or less) privileged than others. In the name of candor and fairness, it is time for Americans to say to legal secularists today what had to be said to Protestants earlier: "Separationist, separate thyself."

Third, legal secularists betray a faulty view of toleration. Toleration is unquestionably an admirable by-product of the broad liberal movement that grew up in reaction to the Wars of Religion, and an infinite improvement on its opposite—intolerance. But toleration has morphed beyond recognition, and today often flip-flops into intolerance again.

For a start, toleration originally assumed clear commitment to a belief. Such a belief was held to strongly, along with toleration for other beliefs considered naive or wrong but tolerated because of the fact of human flaws and therefore of the fallibility of one's own belief. Today, however, toleration has degenerated into intolerance toward any clearly held beliefs, all of which are derided and dismissed as "judg-mental" and "intolerant."

Besides, as Madison and the founders knew well, tolera-tion was always a less effective safeguard for liberty than the positive right of "free exercise." The reason is that toleration can easily become a form of condescension by the strong to the weak, by the government to the citizen, by the majority to the minority—and by those who consider themselves enlight-ened to those they consider ignorant (for example, the ab-surdly self-professed secularist "brights" to the presumed religious "dummies").

Such poisonous condescension has seeped into main-stream American liberalism, which views tolerance as part of a view of public life based on an enlightened rational consen-sus to which all reasonable people will subscribe. Dawkins, for example, displays a stunning arrogance when he de-scribes extremists as "people whose religious faith takes them *right outside the enlightened consensus of my 'moral Zeitgeist'* [italics added]."[13] What this means in practice is that when the secular, liberal way of life is enthroned in public life, all other ways of seeing things are excluded as intolerant and ex-tremist or restricted to the private sphere.

In fact, the Enlightenment notion of a "rational consen-sus," or an overarching rational standard of adjudication agreeable to all, is a fiction. There never has been, and there never will be, any rational consensus subscribed to by all reasonable people about what is the best way to live—least of all in modern pluralistic societies—unless this is taken to mean a consensus to which all good liberals subscribe. To be human is to have deep and abiding differences with other humans over worldviews and values. And, to underscore the point again, such differences are not private worldviews but *entire ways of life* that demand to be lived and heard as freely as the liberal and secularist ways of life. There are issues that cannot be settled by an appeal to reason or tradition, or by any higher standard common to all. As John Gray observes, "Contrary to the liberal idea of toleration, the fact of divergent ways of life is not a result of the frailty of reason. It embodies the truth that humans have reason to live differently."[14]

In short, liberal talk of toleration and rational consensus is often fraudulent—though unwittingly so. It once again ends as a cover for the unofficial establishment of liberalism, and the cause of a curious liberal hypocrisy over diversity. Liberals trumpet the importance of diversity, but their commitment to diversity is no more consistent than nineteenth-century Protestant commitment to religious liberty for those who were not Protestant. In both cases, the principal victims of their selective toleration, also known as intolerance, are people with real differences from them. Liberals end up discounting the seriousness of difference and trashing the very diversity they tout.

Tom Paine, who is so often cited as the patron saint of secularism, was in fact nearer the mark: "Toleration is not the *opposite* of intoleration, but it is the *counterfeit* of it. Both are despotisms. The one assumes to itself the right of withholding liberty of conscience, and the other of granting it."[15]

Fourth, legal secularism is a denial of the principle of self-determination that lies behind human rights such as freedom of conscience and freedom of speech. Fundamental to personhood and to freedom is the conviction of a free and responsible mind, and therefore the ability to think for ourselves, to define ourselves, and to act true to ourselves. Human rights therefore confer the freedom to be and to do what we believe is natural and right for us as humans.

Thus unintentionally but no less drastically, liberals demean human personhood when they invite people freely into the public square, but only on the condition that they leave their faith behind—in other words, when liberals ask religious believers to jettison the deepest source that makes them who they are.

Jewish liberals should understand this point well, because it parallels the first half of the infamous Enlightenment double bind that cruelly confronted Jews in nineteenth-century Europe. Debating the eligibility of Jews for citizenship after the French Revolution, the Comte de Clermont-Tonnerre set out the terms: "The Jews should be denied everything as a nation, but granted everything as individuals.... If they do not want this, they must inform us, and we shall then be compelled to expel them."[16] He was saying, in short, "Become like us or be gone—but the more you become like us, the more you see what makes us who we are, and the more you see that you are forever different." If the dominant party creates the rules on its own terms, the very rules that define membership also define the outsider.

The extreme cruelty for the Jew was that there was no escape from Jewishness, and the double bind led with demonic logic to Hitler's "final solution" to the "Jewish question." For other religious believers, there is always the option of escape through unfaithfulness. But for those who are loyal to their faith, integrity requires they remain true to the vision that makes them who they are, and in the public square no less than the private sphere.

In the name of a classless society, the Soviets once confined ethnic minorities to colorful but innocuous folk festivals. In the name of the Manifest Destiny of the free, nineteenth-century Americans once drove Native American Indians into separate reservations.

In the same way, the present alliance of secularists, strict separationists, and liberal proceduralists restricts religious believers to the segregated margins of private life on behalf of their self-interested liberal myth of a neutral public square. "Public reason" is the respectable alias for secularism, and all religious beliefs are unmasked as "private prejudices." Only the religiously naked and bare, their religious identities stripped down and disinfected in the constitutional neutrality showers, are allowed to enter the naked public square, where the liberal reigns supreme—and remains fully clothed and in command with his constitutional bullwhip.

Where is the justice in this? Between the German death camps and the American naked public square lies a chasm that is morally and physically immeasurable, but the difference is one of degree, not kind.

Liberals who carelessly pick up the charge that Christian conservatives are like Ku Klux Klansmen should look in the mirror with care. History shows an all too close tie-in between the rhetoric of church-state separation and the waves of Know-Nothing nativism and anti-Catholic bigotry. It would be outrageous and quite wrong to suggest that strict separationists are nativist. But the fact is that many were, including one of the leading architects of strict separationism—Justice Hugo Black—who was certainly a Baptist, but also a member of the Alabama Ku Klux Klan and virulently anti-Catholic.

For many separationists, then and now, separationism is a handy way of suppressing religious beliefs with which one disagrees and keeping them out of the mainstream of American life. As such, it should be no part of the philosophy or the policies of liberals who truly champion freedom. The historian Michael Burleigh notes that in Europe secular intellectuals such as Régis Debray and Umberto Eco are now coming to the defense of the Christian faith against silly and politically correct attempts to deny or marginalize it. "There also seems no rational reason," he adds, "to exclude Christians—to range no further—from political debate, any more than there is to deny the vote to people with blue eyes or red hair."[17]

Fifth, legal secularism undermines cultural legitimacy, including the founders' view of sustainable freedom. The founders' view of the relationship of faith and freedom is unique in history and essential to their view of how to sustain freedom. If freedom requires virtue, and virtue requires faith, and faith requires freedom, then the "free exercise" of religion is the absolute prerequisite of sustainable freedom. For the republic, this is a matter not simply of freedom but of self-preservation.

The theory of strict separation blithely ignores the founders' concerns for sustaining freedom and turns the First Amendment on its head. Instead of the No Establishment clause being in support of the Free Exercise clause, and both being in support of greater freedom, No Establishment comes to dominate Free Exercise, and "freedom of religion" sooner or later becomes "freedom from religion." In the process, the founders' view of sustainable freedom is rendered impossible and the inevitable decline of the republic is set in motion.

Originally, both religious-liberty clauses were designed as a check on government, and specifically on the Congress; and they should be understood in the same spirit as the guarantee of freedom of speech. As the constitutional scholar Daniel Driesbach points out, "The free press guarantee was not written to protect the civil state from the press, but to protect a free and independent press from control by the national government."[18] And so it was with religious liberty.

Put differently, when it comes to sustaining freedom, secular liberalism has a "hole in the heart" of its view of national legitimacy. By abandoning both the earlier understanding of "free exercise" and "toleration," and by switching to the principles of strict neutrality and impartiality, the liberal vision has no commitment to virtue of any kind at the center of its free society. The assumption is that liberal society needs only rules and procedures, and has no need for any enduring shared values.

The result is that the strict legal disestablishment of religion is compounded by an equally strict legal disestablishment of morality. The public square is restricted to competing interests that are morally neutral, and morals are confined to the private sphere. Thus the deep wellsprings of American common life are slowly poisoned through a thousand lawsuits, the oxygen supply that is the lifeblood of America's civil society is choked off, and the wise arts of public life are hollowed out and reduced to skills in manipulating the rules. The result is a sure recipe either for hypocrisy (latter-day puritans are as zealous about medical matters, such as smoking, as earlier puritans were about moral matters) or for the folly that Lincoln warned against as a "free people's suicide."[19]

There are obvious ways of ducking the force of the founders' provisions for sustaining freedom: "They were not serious"; "They were only children of their times"; "We have something better able to do the job"; "They were hypocritical"; and so on. But it would be foolish in the extreme to abandon their provision out of ignorance and carelessness. Americans today are free to disagree with their founders' provisions, but they would be wise to be sure first of what it was their founders were trying to do, and then to make sure that they have a better solution to the same problem.

Sixth, legal secularism represents a growing resort to law and a reliance on a language of rights, both of which mean a severe undermining of democratic politics and a steady politicization of law. The rule of law, the primacy of essential rights, and the role of the Constitution as the bulwark of freedom and order are all essential to the American republic, but they in no way contradict the equal right of the American people to debate and decide their public affairs. But the recent resort to law, litigation, judicial activism, and constitutional amendment is shifting the balance so that politics and democracy are the losers. By their very nature, rights and constitutional provisions are universal, final, unconditional, and nonnegotiable; and therefore they are quite unsuitable for deciding the deep differences that make up the divisions in the culture wars—unless accompanied by adequate political debate, negotiation, compromise, and allowance for regional variation.

Premature resort to law alone is itself a legal form of intolerance, because of the way it bypasses politics and short-circuits debate among citizens. Ironically, it leads to a politicization of law, which in turn lessens the detachment that law needs, and works to supplant politics by law.

Worse still, by using law to bypass political debate and to decide such morally contentious issues as the right to abortion and the nature of marriage, judicial activism (whether by liberals or conservatives) ends only in making the religiously incommensurable into the politically intractable and the socially irreconcilable. It therefore exacerbates the culture warring already destroying America's civil peace and sapping her civil strength. Better far to trust the messy business of debate, negotiation, and compromise, which are the bread and butter of democratic politics and prudential realism.

Seventh, legal secularism often produces unintended consequences that are highly illiberal. If strict separation is used as a tool for legal secularism rather than as a promotion of freedom for all, the results often boomerang on their users. Alternatively, if religious liberty is viewed merely as liberty for the religious, only religious believers will worry about "freedom of religion" becoming "freedom from religion." But the consequences of shortchanging religious liberty do not stop with religious believers or with religious liberty, and all who care for freedom should note some of the ironies of how liberalism becomes illiberal and even antihumanist.

One of the loudest lessons of the history of liberty is that yesterday's oppressed often become today's oppressors. In the famous indictment of John Milton, today's "new Presbyter is but old priest writ large."[20] Or in Roger Williams's tirade against the inconsistency and hypocrisy of the Boston Puritans who supported Queen Elizabeth's persecution of the Catholics but criticized King James's persecution of the Puritans: "One weight for themselves when they are under hatches, and another for others when they come to the helm."[21]

The reason for such hypocrisies lies in the dynamic nature of freedom, the twisted timber of our humanity, and the selective and self-interested way in which we use and abuse freedom. Take the fact of the general hostility and intolerance that so often mark liberal and secularist discussions of religion. They are the buried consequences, it is said, of the widespread liberal and secularist repression of religion, but they should make true liberals pause to think.

Or take the more specific tactic of some gay rights activists who believe that the justice of their cause trumps the principle of religious liberty. (There are certainly gay rights activists who disagree with this view.) For the first time in American history, they have divided civil liberty from religious liberty and elevated the former at the expense of the latter by expanding the elastic notion of "discrimination." Gays and lesbians have been oppressed, and so, they argue, their rights needed to be recognized and protected as a matter of civil liberty, whatever the consequences for religious liberty. But what these activists did next was a sleight of hand that played the civil liberty card in order to trump religious liberty, and thus made conscience-based *differences* into matters of *discrimination*.

Arguing that all who differed with them on the basis of religious liberty were "homophobes" and "heterosexists," and therefore guilty of discrimination, prejudice, and intolerance, these activists went on to charge that who disagreed with them were guilty of "hate speech." Under such pressure, for example, many eminent universities and colleges, including Tufts, Rutgers, and the University of North Carolina, responded by banning religious groups who differed with homosexual behavior on grounds of conscience and would not allow practicing homosexuals to be elected leaders in their organizations.

Many of these ill-considered university decisions have been reversed. And not surprisingly so, because their direction was absurd, and would have been seen so at once to a generation better acquainted with the history of religious liberty and more attuned to the challenges of freedom and justice. For a start, "discrimination" is far from simple and unambiguous, as the positive word "discriminating" signifies, so it is bad day for ethics when all disagreements can be labeled as discrimination. Then, too, "hate speech" is a clumsy weapon with which to fight prejudice, because it presumes we have a knowledge of each other's motives as humans, motives that are actually impenetrable and impossible to assess objectively. But if "hate" is in the eye of the beholder, then "hate speech" (and "hate crimes") are a weapon in the hands of the power wielder, and a constant danger to the rights of minorities or those whose views are out of favor.

Woe betide anyone caught with the merest deviation from the canons of the orthodoxy and political correctness of the day, for their "discrimination" makes them vulnerable to the charge of a "hate speech." Well-intended but misguided, the idea of "hate speech" is a recent liberal tactic that ends in illiberalism. As Pope Benedict XVI warns, "A confused ideology of liberty leads to a dogmatism that is proving ever more hostile to real liberty."[22]

Liberals truly concerned with freedom would be wiser to understand and employ the positive principles of freedom of conscience and the free exercise of faith. When prejudice and hate have their way, it is wiser and more realistic to protect the liberties they threaten than to use law to try to purge all traces of the evil they represent.

Equally important, civil liberty should never be allowed to trump religious liberty so carelessly. "Free exercise" means that groups as well as individuals are free to decide on the basis of conscience what they believe and what their beliefs mean for their identity, membership, and ways of life. It is therefore only natural and proper for each faith community to accept into membership, and especially into leadership, only those who are in line with their beliefs. Such defining beliefs are conscience-based distinctions about the meaning and ordering of life, distinctions that they believe are "discriminating" rather than "discrimination."

Do synagogues have to accept Christians into membership or be accused of discrimination? Are mosques required to welcome atheists, Buddhists, and Scientologists? No more so than the Democratic Party must accept Republicans, the ACLU Klansmen, or the American Association of Retired People teenagers—and no more so than Orthodox Jews must accept Roman Catholics or evangelicals must accept into their leadership those with whose beliefs and behavior they disagree.

To put the point like that shows the absurdity of the argument. But the same logic that drives the homosexual tactic means that James Madison's *free exercise,* so boldly inserted in the Virginia Declaration of Rights as a far better concept than John Locke's *toleration,* is stopped dead in its tracks, or shunted off to a sandbox. By such power tactics, those who disagree with religious differences of any sort can twist them and portray them as *discrimination,* and when they do so, what starts out as protecting a way of life slides across into *promoting* one way of life at the expense of others.

In short, if freedom is to be just, indivisible, and a matter of equality for all, then religious liberty and civil liberty must be considered together and must be viewed as matters of principle, not as power plays, and balanced judiciously against each other. Otherwise, the iron law of unintended consequences unfolds:

The liberal pursuit of liberty for some ends in the illiberal denying of liberty and diversity for others.

The liberal desire for negative freedom, freedom from interference, becomes a grand and dangerous form of positive freedom and an illiberal interference into the lives of others.

The liberal passion for tolerance all of a sudden becomes intolerant, and the liberal dream of diversity ends in conformism and uniformity through the rise of political correctness: "Anybody who is not like everybody is a nobody, and must be denied a voice."

When we are offered freedom but required to join the majority in order to be truly free, we are not so much free as seduced into conformity. As always, the pursuit of liberty for selfish and selective ends, as a matter of power rather than principle, ends in illiberalism, even if the perpetrators are liberals. The old priest becomes the new presbyter who in turn becomes a new proselytizer for a new political correctness. The result is the de facto establishment of yet another orthodoxy—secular and more modern, to be sure, but no less intolerant.

Doubtless it takes a special courage for liberals to fight liberal illiberalism, just as it takes a special courage for conservatives to break ranks with the follies and errors of their conservative compatriots. But justice and liberty are not mocked. The first principles of freedom and the times in which we live demand no less—of people on both sides.

Chapter Six

A Cosmopolitan
and Civil Public Square

I have always been fascinated by one of the least noticed but most intriguing items at one of America's most visited tourist sites—the key of the Bastille at George Washington's home, Mount Vernon. The Bastille was the forbidding Paris fortress that symbolized the grim repression of the ancien régime under the Bourbons, so that the date of its fall, July 14, 1789, became the day on which the French celebrate independence. Along with the Marseillaise and *le drapeau tricolor*, the storming of the Bastille became one of the great symbols of the French Revolution.

Heavy and far from Georgian elegant, the massive key hangs in the hall at Mount Vernon, oversized and underappreciated. Just as Jefferson had welcomed the French Revolution as the successor to and partner of the American Revolution, so the Marquis de Lafayette had taken the key of the Bastille in 1789 and sent it to his good friend Washington as the symbol of their common hopes for revolutionary freedom.

Needless to say, both Jefferson's and Lafayette's hopes for France were dashed, as they were both sobered by the reign of terror and the revolutionary tyranny that erupted under the malign though different influences of Robespierre, Danton, and Napoleon. As Gouverneur Morris, the U.S. ambassador to France, wrote home in disgust four days before the Bastille was stormed, "They want an American Constitution with the exception of a king instead of a President, without reflecting that they have no Americans to uphold that constitution."[1]

Two centuries later, that discussion sounds remarkably fresh as the United States recoils from the fiasco of its democracy-building in Iraq. Is it any more realistic to export democracy than it was to copy a revolution? Can people be forced to be free or even helped to be free when they neither have reached the optimum stage of economic progress nor have the required strength of cultural values? Is it enough to have free, fair elections, with all the paraphernalia of ballot boxes and international observers, while not having essentials such as the notions of the rule of law, freedom of conscience, individual human dignity, and human rights?

Opinions differ sharply over these issues, with conservatives as divided from neoconservatives as both are from liberals. But what is odd in an era clouded by ethnic and sectarian violence is that no part of the American experiment stands out more clearly as a key to solving modern troubles than the religious-liberty clauses of the First Amendment, yet no part is less appreciated or copied—simply because Americans themselves are not living up to the promise of their founders' provision.

Restoring the Civil Public Square

If neither of the two existing visions—the *sacred public square* and the *naked public square*—does justice to the genius of the founders' vision and the challenges of today's world, is there a better way, an alternative to waging the culture wars to the bitter end? Is there a way that fosters the interests of liberty, diversity, equality, and harmony at the same time? Is there a "virtuous circle" to offset the "vicious circle" we have just seen? I believe the way forward lies in a vision of a cosmopolitan society and a civil public square.

The vision of a civil public square is one in which everyone—people of all faiths, whether religious or naturalistic—are equally free to enter and engage public life on the basis of their faiths, as a matter of "free exercise" and as dictated by their own reason and conscience; but always within the double framework, first, of the Constitution, and second, of a freely and mutually agreed covenant, or common vision for the common good, of what each person understands to be just and free for everyone else, and therefore of the duties involved in living with the deep differences of others.

The first half of this definition simply restates the primacy and equality of religious liberty for all citizens, whereas the second half points to the framework needed for a new way of understanding religious liberty in the changed conditions of our contemporary world, one that promotes civility and harmony rather than tension and conflict.

Put differently, the vision of a civil public square rests on two foundational premises, one of which is theoretical and one practical. First, the principle of religious liberty for all rests on and requires an essential mutuality, or reciprocity, of rights, responsibilities, and respect—the "three Rs" of religious liberty. Thus a right for one person is a right for another person and a responsibility for both. A right for a Christian is a right for a Jew, and right for an atheist, and a right for a Muslim, and a right for Buddhist, and a right for a Mormon, and a right for a Scientologist, and a right for the adherent of every possible faith or nonfaith within the wide span of the fifty states, either today or in some future as yet unseen. In principle, there is no right for anyone that is not thereby a right for everyone.

Second, the practice of religious liberty for all requires that if the interests of liberty, diversity, equality, and harmony are to be promoted and preserved together, such reciprocal rights require specific understandings of about how differences are to be debated and decided in practice. The Three Rs must be neither left at the level of abstractions nor made subject only to law. They must be specified in a covenant framework, mutually agreed upon, and then taught from generation to generation, so that they become the habits of the heart and the unspoken but powerful, informal rules that guard civility.

For example, take the need for the practice of persuasion in public life. One of the most important practical legacies of the earlier American settlement was the way the First Amendment shifted public discourse about religion from *coercion* to *persuasion*. Americans who yawn at the obviousness of that achievement might pause to remember that genuine democratic persuasion was an early casualty of the culture wars. As I said, the two sides often do not engage with each other at all. They do not talk to the other side; they simply talk about the other side to their own side.

This lack of persuasion in American public life has become chronic. Many current arguments about such hot-button issues as abortion and same-sex marriage remind me of Grant Wood's famous painting, *American Gothic*. Short, stout, simplistic summary statements are staked defiantly into the ground like a pitchfork, with no attempt to see if they are intelligible or appealing and persuasive to anyone else. The language of protest, pronouncement, and proclamation has almost completely replaced the language of persuasion, and those who make such poor arguments are the losers as well as the republic itself.

The I-Thou Discourse of the Grand Republic

Stated simply and left at that, the vision of a civil public square would be easy to dismiss, an easily caricatured ideal for partisans of one extreme or another to shoot at. But thoughtful citizens would be wise to ponder some of the underlying assumptions and their significance.

First, the vision of a civil public square both supports and supplements the Constitution, though it insists that law alone, and certainly not the Constitution alone, will never bring an end to America's culture warring, let alone settle the deepest issues of religious liberty and diversity in American society.

There are certainly things that only the law can do. I, for one, support Noah Feldman's brilliantly simple proposal that the way forward for interpreting the Constitution is to "offer greater latitude for public religious discourse and religious symbolism, and at the same time insist on a stricter ban on state funding of religious institutions and activities." In sum, that the Constitution should be interpreted in the direction of "no coercion and no money."[2]

But law and litigation alone will never be enough to resolve the culture warring. They are necessary but not sufficient. To rely on them alone will lead to more and more convoluted and unsatisfactory decisions, and eventually it will subvert the authority of the Constitution itself. At best the law is a club rather than a scalpel, and no one who has studied the course of constitutional interpretation of the First Amendment over the last fifty years can fail to see the overall incoherence of the Supreme Court's decisions. Indeed, if Jefferson's "wall of separation" is as wavy as his serpentine walls, at least they are both elegantly so. The same cannot be said for court decisions that more often resemble the path of a drunken sailor.

The disarray of the Supreme Court has been widely commented on, not least by the Supreme Court itself, with the liberals, conservatives, and moderates all bewailing the incoherence in their turn. Justice Anthony Kennedy, for example, bluntly warned that the court's approach to the No Establishment clause was "flawed in its fundamentals and unworkable in practice."[3]

To be fair, the courts have been asked to do what neither Moses, Solon, nor the angel Gabriel could ever do, and that no court in the world can ever do. There are issues that are better not taken to law, conflicts that are better resolved through custom, civility, common sense, compromise, and political debate rather than by the courts—in a word, by a restoration of Tocqueville's celebrated "habits of the heart" and by a renewal in our changed conditions of what I have called the American settlement.

Second, the vision of a civil public square is a conscious reforging of the ancient Jewish notion of covenant that already underlies the Constitution, and of the classical notion of a republic. As such, it is not simply a form of pluralism, or even "principled pluralism," but a genuine form of covenant pluralism or chartered pluralism—that is, a vision of pluralism within the bounds of a freely chosen covenant or charter.

Alexander Hamilton opened the first of the Federalist Papers with his famous assertion that Americans could "decide the important question, whether societies of men are really capable or not of establishing good government from reflection and choice, or whether they are forever destined to depend for their political constitutions on accident and force."[4] He was saying what many historians and political scientists have argued: that nations and other political groups come into existence in three ways—through conquest, organic development, or covenant—and that the different origins determine the different outcomes for the nation in many decisive ways.

According to the historian and theorist of covenants Daniel J. Elazar, a political covenant involves a coming together of basically equal humans through a mutually and morally binding pact, supported by reference to a power that transcends all of them, thus establishing among the partners a new framework or setting them on the road to a new task that can be dissolved only by a mutual agreement of all the parties.

As Elazar outlines it, the seminal idea of covenant that broke into the world powerfully in the Jewish experience resurfaced in the Protestant Reformation, and then again in the New England Puritans and through them in the U.S. Constitution and the attempt to form "a more perfect union" in 1787. Unlike the other two avenues of conquest and organic development, covenant is a particularly apt way to order society for people who want to be free and who are starting out fresh. Obviously, the leaders of the American Revolution were not conquerors and were starting out from scratch in frontier conditions—by reflection, by choice, and by a freely chosen and mutually binding covenant.

This notion of covenant and consent, and its debt to the Jews, has been overshadowed in the last century. From one side, it has been obscured by a concentration on natural law rather than covenant, and from the other on positive, secular law rather than covenant. The result is that law has become all-important, the decisions of the law courts have become all-decisive, and the place of agreement and consent, and therefore of a common vision for the common good, has become all but irrelevant. In the process, companion notions such as "freely chosen consent," "mutually binding compact," "under God," and their own companion notions such as "the cultivation of the habits of the heart" and "the American way" have been hollowed out and reduced to the point of disappearance.

This neglect makes the task of rebuilding a civil public square harder than ever, for what was once strong but implicit and unspoken has now collapsed. It must therefore be rebuilt carefully and explicitly, and rebuilt in the same arena in which the culture wars are being fought.

Third, this vision of a civil public square is a necessary complement to today's talk of a civil society. Republicanism to the founders was not a party, or even a particular form of government; it was a government constituted for the *res publica,* "the public thing" or the common good. Thus a republic or country is healthy, it is said, when it has a vital civil society that serves the interests of the public good—when between the countless individuals who make up the society and the government that rules it are multiple layers of autonomous, intermediary associations, the "little platoons" in which citizens can volunteer, participate, give of their time, talent, and treasure, and generally place their trust.

Too much interference by the state above or too much indifference from the citizens below, and civil society will be cramped from above or cut off from its oxygen supply from below. The outcome in either case will be a deficit of freedom, as well as of human giving, caring, and engagement.

Expressed differently, a healthy civil society may be attacked or eroded from two directions, especially if the two combine to form a pincer movement. Obviously civil society can be oppressed from the top by what Hannah Arendt called the "totalitarian tendency," or in liberal societies by forms of political correctness that stifle the freedom and diversity of unwelcome opinion and activities—an attitude that has been called "totalitolerance." But it can equally be undermined from below by forms of thought and action that are better kept at the level of the private and personal. For example, the collapse of the public square, and "the fall of public man," have led to "identity politics," "lifestyle politics," and a rash of politicized scandals, all of which are an explosion into public life of issues once considered the realm of the private.

In short, civil society can be eroded from above by forces that are *unwelcoming* to liberty and diversity, and from below by forces that are *unworthy* of the public life of free peoples.

All existing societies fall short of the "good society" of our ideals and dreams. But we who are citizens of liberal democracies count on the state to do for us certain things that are clear but limited, and then to leave us free, both as individuals and as groups, to choose the ways of life we prefer.

Civil society is therefore a grand and continuing exercise in balancing government and society on the one hand, and unity and diversity on the other, thus cultivating a healthy freedom that keeps the balance. For freedom is best guaranteed not by speeches and declarations, and not simply by laws, but by our vigorous pursuit of the visions we owe to ourselves and the duties we owe to our fellow citizens. Thus voluntary organizations such as the Girl Scouts, Rotary, and the Red Cross, and all the voluntary acts of giving, caring, engagement, and participation that they encourage, have two important functions. They create the lifeblood of civil society and are the surest way to accumulate social capital; and they are also the best way to keep the government at bay and so to sustain the vitality of freedom.

Yet here is a point often overlooked. *A vision of a healthy civil society assumes and requires the construction of a civil public square.* It has been said that thriving civility in public life is the equivalent of mature I-Thou relationships in private life. In Elazar's words, covenantal ties are "the concretization of the relationship of dialogue, which, when addressed to God, makes humans holy, and when addressed to one's peers, makes people human" (and therefore, we might add, respected fellow citizens).[5]

If that is true, there is a gaping hole in much of America's discussion today that is dehumanizing as well as decivilizing: claims for a civil society have been trumpeted, whereas talk of a civil public square has been derided. But without a civil public square there will be no civil society in the end, for an uncivil public square and a civil society are at odds with each other. In the last chapter, the issue was the illiberalism that denied the integrity of people of faith. Here the same point is put more positively: the "I-Thou" requirements of true civil discourse mean that each of us who talks and debates with others does so with the full integrity of who we are, and not as neutered by some illiberal demand that we drop the faith that is the core of who we are and the animating vision by which we see the world.

Historically, discussion of civility has always lagged behind discussion of civil society. Today we are paying for that neglect, and civility must be recovered among liberals as much as among those that liberals consider extreme and uncouth. Unless we are each able to speak freely for ourselves and negotiate our differences with others and with the government, we confront what the sociologist Zygmunt Bauman has called "one of the most notorious of the notoriously unsquarable circles"—preserving the liberty of the individual, the government, and the group "while making the liberty of each a condition of the freedom of others."[6]

No, Not That

For many people, all such positive considerations about a civil public square are outweighed by certain negative apprehensions, born of fears and misunderstandings. Three dismissals in particular are common.

First, some people resist the notion of a civil public square because they see it as tantamount to civil religion. The term "civil religion" was introduced into mainstream American discussion by Robert Bellah and his celebrated article in *Daedalus* in 1967, but it goes back to Jean-Jacques Rousseau and his discussion of the social contract and how a nation builds its own systems of meaning by its own acts of will. Nations invoke their nation-gods for the nation's good.

It might seem unlikely that a nation so opposed to the establishment of religion as the United States would allow any religion to be given such a place in public life, and even more unlikely that the Christian faith would become entangled with what the historian William Lee Miller has called "a seminationalist religion and a semireligious nationalism."[7] For along with adherents of the other great monotheistic faiths, Judaism and Islam, Christians have always held that there is one God, and no god but God; so God alone is to be wor-shipped. Augustine, for instance, denounced Roman civil theology as "idolatrous," and Rousseau recognized the essen-tial incompatibility of the Christian faith and civil religion when he said that the notion of a "Christian republic" is self-contradictory, because the two terms are mutually exclusive.

Yet over the course of time the United States has given rise to its own soft civil religion, and the reason lies in the charac-ter and function of civil religion. In the absence of an official religion, what binds a nation together becomes suffused with a sense of the sacred and surrounded with a religious or semireligious aura until it becomes its civil religion. Thus, in essence, civil religion is a nation's worship of itself.

In the case of the United States, its vibrant liberty and di-versity put added pressure on the search for a sure *unum* to balance its strong *pluribus*. America therefore had to find this unity and steer a course between the founders' decisive ban on any established orthodoxy and their equally decisive judg-ment that public life without any ideals was dangerous. The result was a blending of patriotism with a diluted and gener-alized Protestantism that formed a moderate and highly un-usual form of American civil religion. Theologically and constitutionally speaking, American national unity and stabil-ity have never depended on the common sharing of one faith, but practically speaking, for many Americans they have, and the themes of patriotism have been given a religious glow. As the historian David Fischer points out, male images of Amer-ica such as Uncle Sam and Yankee Doodle have always been popular, but the most appealing image of all has always been the timeless female goddess of liberty.[8]

Resistance to civil religion comes from two sides. On the one hand, many secularists and some Jews are suspicious of civil religion because they view it as a way to escort religion, and especially the unquestioned place of religion in the past, back into public life with an armed escort and a color guard.

This suspicion is justified. Wrap any American issue in the flag, and those who differ with it are unpatriotic and un-American. Christian conservatives therefore need to be patriots with independent consciences and critical minds, and to be vigilant in their guard against any uncritical shift from legitimate patriotism to nationalism, for nationalism is another example of where the fundamentalism of the Religious Right is modern rather than Christian.

On the other hand, many Christians themselves are even more opposed to civil religion than secularists are. For if God alone is to be worshipped, then the worship of anything short of God is idolatry, especially if civil religion means that Christians are essentially worshipping themselves. Political freedom, for example, is a gift, a precious gift and a privilege; but for Christians, political freedom is and will always remain a secular gift. It is not sacred and it is not God, so to sing, as the American hymn does, of "freedom's holy light," and to think and act as if such were the case, is to cross the line into civil religion and idolatry.

Against all such confusions and misunderstandings, it must be stated unambiguously that a civil public philosophy is secular; it is not a civil religion, and it must never be elevated into being religious. A civil public philosophy is a matter of the common vision for the common good, the shared agreement about the rights, responsibilities, and respect that form the common bonds within which Americans can live freely and debate important differences. This common vision is an achievement and a gift. For some it is a gift from God as well as a legacy from the past, while for others it is simply a legacy from the past; but for neither is it religious or a matter of civil religion.

The Myth of the Common Core

Second, some people resist the notion of a civil public philosophy because of its confusion with the search for a common core or the lowest common denominator. Needless to say, the desired goal is admirable: to handle differences with civility rather than resorting to conflict. But here we come to an important fork in the road. There are two different ways to work for civility, and one of them, though attractive because personal, is in the end limited and ineffective.

The first approach is to search for common ground, for a common core of unity that is presumed to underlie all our human differences, including religious differences. If only, say the proponents of this approach, we show enough goodwill to each other, and talk long enough to each other, we will arrive at a place of uncomplicated, pure humanity that lies below all our differences. For some, this approach is religiously motivated; for others, it is politically motivated. For some, the goal of the common core is considered feasible; for others the end is unlikely, though the means are still made worthwhile by the TINA principle—"There is no alternative." But for whatever motive and with whatever prospects, those who search for the common core of unity are intent on doing their part through patient and determined dialogue.

Such dialogue is valuable as far as it goes. It is rarely wasted, and it occasionally creates a breakthrough through which undreamed-of forms of reconciliation and peace are possible. But as an overall project on behalf of civility in public life, the quest is forlorn for a simple reason: *there is no common core, and there is no all-inclusive identity.*

To be blunt, there is no universal human language. There is no reason common to all humans. There is no agreed rational consensus of values. There is no scientific and universally valid philosophy. There is no humanity without borders. There is no Parliament of Man or Federation of the World. There is no all-inclusive form of identity that will embrace everyone without exception. There is no final form of universal civilization toward which history will progress. There is no pure humanity beyond complexity, and no unity below all human diversity. All these ideas are utopian longings that die hard. They are no more realizable than the ancient dream of Babel and more modern Enlightenment dreams such as perpetual peace, world democracy, and a single global free market.

We can talk as long as we like, and be as nice to each other as we can be, but we shall never find a common core of truth on which all good humans will agree. Americanization, Westernization, and modernization can no more flatten the world's diversity today than Alexander the Great and Charlemagne could earlier. In our faiths and languages and cultures, we are diverse to the core.

We humans will always have different worldviews and different ways of life, and at some points these differences will always be religiously irreducible, philosophically incommensurable, and politically intractable. Which means that we are all always fated to live between two worlds, our own and those of others. We will all always live between the two poles of the global and the local, the inclusive and the particular. We will all always need to be bilingual: translators, negotiators, and persuaders. In the words of Ulrich Beck, we will all always have to have "both roots and wings."[9]

In fact, when it comes to our religiously grounded differences, our differences are ultimate and most irreducible—which is precisely why our core question is, How do we live with our deepest differences, especially when those differences are the religiously and ideologically grounded differences of entire ways of life?

The plain fact is that we shall never, and can never, transcend all our human differences. What divides us will always be as deep as, if not deeper than, what unites us. And beyond that: not only are our religious and ideological differences ultimate and irreducible; they are important and consequential because all such differences make a difference—and not only for individuals but for societies and even civilizations. Differences therefore need to be debated; and as John Courtney Murray points out, disagreements are an achievement, and the way we discuss and debate our differences is crucial to anyone pursuing the notion of a good society and the rich benefits of a diverse society.[10]

To be sure, there are important ways of balancing diversity and negotiating our differences so that we are not reduced to a Hobbesian war of all against all. There are, for example, important commonalities between different members of the same family of faiths, such as the likenesses between Hinduism and Buddhism or between Judaism and the Christian faith. Or again, even in deeply diverse societies such as the United States, there are solid reasons why it is possible to achieve an "overlapping consensus" that provides a point of unity to balance the deep diversity, the *unum* to offset the *pluribus.*

But none of these approaches add up to success in the quest for the common core, and a quite different, second approach is more fruitful. *The better approach is to pursue civility not through searching for a rational consensus or a mythical common core but through setting up a mutually agreed-upon framework, or covenant, or charter, within which important differences can be negotiated and settled peacefully.* What we are looking for is not so much truths that can unite us as terms on which we can negotiate and by which we can live with the differences that divide us.

In John Gray's words, the way forward is to search for a means of coexistence rather than for a consensus, a modus vivendi rather than a universal agreement, an "agonistic" or competitive liberalism rather than a consensual liberalism.[11] In John Courtney Murray's words, the point of unity we must establish is an "article of peace," not an "article of faith."[12] At the level of faiths, our differences will always be deep, irreducible, and incompatible.

Numerous possible errors confront Americans at this stage of the controversies over religious liberty. One is to be overconfident and therefore complacent about America's capacity to handle diversity. Jefferson was right when he wrote to Jacob De La Motta that "religious freedom is the most effective anodyne against religious dissension" and that when it comes to religion the normal maxims of civil government are reversed: with religion, "divided we stand, united we fall."[13]

But this capacity needs to be guarded with care. George Orwell argued famously that Jefferson's "Truth is great and shall prevail" is now more a prayer than an axiom, and the question has been raised today as to whether nations can reach the outer limits of diversity. So two things are critical: first, that all faiths really are experiencing religious liberty; and second, that the bonds of unity are strengthened as the boundaries of diversity are stretched.

Another potential error is to duck the problems of particularity in the public square by trying to deal with religion only through ecumenical and interfaith coalitions and organizations—as if that would be safer and less controversial than dealing with the prickly problems of particular faiths. In faith-based funding, for example, the temptation is to reduce faith to social work and look to interreligious coalitions rather than to organizations that have a clear and particular faith. (When a reporter referred to her sisters as social workers, Mother Teresa replied: "We are not social workers. We do this for Jesus.") Or again, ABC television switched from its pioneering religion correspondent, who was superbly professional in her objectivity but a person of faith, and made much of their announced reliance for their religious news on an organization that was "ecumenical."

The nervousness about controversy is understandable, but the reluctance to think and act according to first principles is lamentable. Religious liberty is for particular faiths and particular individuals, not for generic religion. Better a controversial but genuine success in drug rehabilitation than a thousand inoffensive failures. Better a smart professionally objective reporter, be he or she Christian, Jewish, atheist, Muslim, or Mormon, than a hundred safe and dull news sources.

Properly understood and rightly ordered, diversity and particularity are not a matter of weakness, but strength. Playing safe through what is often a pale and diluted unity becomes self-defeating. Such milquetoast diffidence discourages individual passion, constricts real diversity, and blocks what is often the real secret of an individual's or an organization's success—the power of their faith in all its stubborn particularity.

Yet another potential error is for Americans to confuse civility with niceness, as if civility were a higher form of manners fit for a Victorian dinner or a Japanese tea cere-mony. With some people, this error flows from a genuine misunderstanding; with others, it is a cover: they are leery of the hard work of respect-forged civility and frankly relish any excuse for a good old-fashioned shoot-out or no-holds-barred slugfest.

No arguments will persuade the latter, short of the futility and failure of their ways of operating, but the former have misunderstood civility. Genuine civility is more than deco-rous public manners, or squeamishness about differences, or a form of freshman sensitivity training. It is substantive be-fore it is formal. It is not a rhetoric of niceness, or a psychol-ogy of adjustment, or a form of conflict prevention. It is a republican virtue that is a matter of principle and a habit of the heart. It is a style of public discourse shaped by respect for the humanity and dignity of individuals, as well as for truth and the common good—and also, in this case, by the American constitutional tradition.

American republicanism, as George Weigel reminds us, is "a system that is built *for* tension."[14] Far from stifling debate, civility helps to strengthen debate because of its respect for truth, yet all the while keeping debate constructive and within bounds because of its respect for the rights of other people and for the common good. Those who are worried about tough, robust civil debate forget what an achievement dis-agreement is, and how creative the contribution of tough, ro-bust civil debate can be.

An apt picture of this second approach to civility—setting up an agreed-upon framework within which differences can be settled robustly—is the ideal of sportsmanship that was the goal of the Queensberry rules in boxing. When the Ninth Marquess of Queensberry lent his name to the Queensberry rules for boxing, boxing was more a drawn-out form of murder than a sport, with bare-knuckle fights that could last a hundred rounds, and boxers who sometimes fought to the death. The Romans, after all, tolerated gladiatorial games, but they banned boxing in A.D. 39 as too brutal.

So what the Queensberry rules did was to put boxing inside a ring, within rules, and under a referee. But while boxers touch gloves at the start of the fight, and are disqualified for such things as punches below the belt during the fight, they still fight, and there are still winners and losers at the end. In sum, boxing was civilized to a degree, and boxers were persuaded that the object was not simply to win, but to win by the rules.

So too with political civility: it is forged within a covenanted framework, or charter, of the three Rs of religious liberty—rights, responsibilities, and respect. But civility is not for wimps; it is competitive. It is first and foremost a matter of political debate rather than an attempt at shortcutting through judicial decision. Important political differences have to be "fought out" in the public square, but the term *fight* is now only a metaphor, and *winners* have their responsibilities as well as *losers* their rights. In other words, political debates are won and lost, and policies and laws come and go, but all within the bounds of what is mutually agreed to be in the interests of the common good. The unthinkable alternative is the no-holds-barred war of all against all.

A tough, robust, principled civility is absolutely vital to America, and to throw it away casually is as irresponsible as it is for Americans to wage war internationally without a sober respect for the consequences of action that is not properly legitimized. In both cases the result is a massive loss of credibility for which America will pay dearly in the long run.

In a celebrated argument between Sir Thomas More and his son-in-law Roper in Robert Bolt's play *A Man for All Seasons* (1960), the younger man is as impatient with Sir Thomas's willingness to give the Devil the benefit of law as many people are today about the place of civility.

"What would he do?" More asks Roper. "Would he cut through the laws to get to the Devil?" When Roper answers that he would cut down every law in England to get after the Devil, More simply asks him what he would do when the forest of laws was flattened and there was no windbreak left. How could he stand upright then? Today's proponents of a careless erosion of civility should ponder More's point.

The Right to Be Wrong

Third, some people resist the notion of a civil public square because they associate it with a false tolerance. The concern behind this position is genuine, though the thinking is confused. Respect a person's right to believe what he or she decides to believe, the argument goes, and you have to accept their position and turn a blind eye to things that are untrue and dangerous. Once a feature of fundamentalist suspicions, this fear can now be heard from secularists. Richard Dawkins writes in *The God Delusion*, "As long as we accept the principle that religious faith must be respected simply because it is religious faith, it is hard to withhold respect from the faith of Osama bin Laden and the suicide bombers. The alternative, one so transparent that it should need no urging, is to abandon the principle of automatic respect for religious faith."[15]

Not so. Dawkins is confusing a person's right to believe something and what it is they believe. And his error lies behind what is an abhorrent feature of the new atheism: its double intolerance and its extremism as a counter to extremism—intolerance of those it considers intolerant as well as intolerance of moderates who tolerate them.

On the one hand, Dawkins is openly intolerant of those he considers religiously deluded—"faithheads"—and his position comes close to the medieval maxim that "error has no rights." "It's one thing to say people should be free to believe whatever it is that they like," he argues, "but should they be free to impose their beliefs on their children? Is there something to be said for society stepping in? What about bringing up children to believe manifest falsehoods?"[16]

Wait a minute. Now who is the one calling for interference and coercion by the state? Religious believers who are that "deluded," Dawkins recommends, should be rescued by the state from passing on their "delusions" to their children. Thus ends the vaunted liberal freedom that was "freedom from interference," and thus grows the power of the state as the great licensing authority for society—in this case, on behalf of atheism. Why is Dawkins cheered as a rock star at American liberal-arts colleges when he espouses such ill-considered notions? Authoritarianism by whatever name should be challenged by all who are genuine liberals.

On the other hand, Dawkins is equally withering in his dismissal of moderates who tolerate those he considers extremists. As one reporter wrote after an interview, "The New Atheists will not let us off the hook simply because we are not doctrinaire believers. They condemn not just belief in God but *respect* for belief in God. Religion is not only wrong; it's evil."[17] Dawkins does not merely disagree with religious myths; he disagrees with tolerating them at all.

On the fundamentalist side, there is the added fear that if they join the side of liberals more tolerant than Dawkins, they will discover that liberal tolerance is selective, and they will find liberals tolerant of everyone except them.

Beware tolerance, we are warned from opposing angles.

Such tangled thinking needs untangling. *Toleration* was certainly the term of choice in matters of religious liberty before American independence. It had been made popular by writings such as John Locke's *A Letter Concerning Toleration* and copied into the first draft of the Virginia Declaration of Rights in 1776 by George Mason. Young James Madison objected, however, and when he succeeded in changing the word *tolerance* to the words *free exercise,* he advanced the cause of religious liberty by light-years. Tolerance is too condescending and uncertain. It is the gesture of the strong toward the weak, the government toward the citizenry, and the majority toward the minority. Free exercise, by contrast, is inalienable because it is the inalienable right of everyone, the minority no less than the majority, the weak as well as the poor, and the citizens just as much as the government.

This sturdy distinction between tolerance and free exercise, condescension and civility, lies at the heart of the American experiment. But it also contains a trap. *"The right to believe anything"* does not mean *"Anything anyone believes is right."* The first part of the sentence is a matter of freedom of conscience, and is absolute and inalienable, whereas the second part is sheer stupidity.

All credit to the ACLU when they support the right of Nazis and homosexual haters such as Pastor Fred Phelps to freedom of conscience and free speech, even though they, and I, consider such views abhorrent. But as such examples show, there are things that people are free to believe that are half-baked, muddle headed, inconsiderate, foolish—or just plain untrue, wrong, and evil. People's right to believe them, and our duty to respect their right, does not mean that they are correct in those beliefs and that we have to accept them.

Respect for freedom of conscience means that, on the one hand, unlike many in the Middle Ages, and Richard Dawkins and the politically correct today, we reject the idea that "error has no rights." Everyone, with no exceptions, has a right to be wrong. The dictates of conscience are inalienable. On the other hand, this negative freedom of "the right to be wrong" has to be counterbalanced by two positive freedoms. For conscience, though inalienable, is not infallible.

First, respect for freedom of conscience, which means submission to the dictates of conscience, means that we have a "responsibility to be right." If there are deep and important differences between people, it is foolish to think that "everyone is right"—which in today's extreme form even becomes "everyone is right except us." If "everyone is right," it is more likely that everyone is wrong, for if we truly differ in our views, some views are likely to be wrong, and in ways that matter.

Thus as human beings who are keenly aware of the prime importance of truth seeking as well as our proven capacity for truth twisting, we not only grant others the right to be wrong, but have a duty ourselves to seek truth above everything. Respecting the right to be wrong does not mean casual indifference toward truth. "Having bought truth dear," Roger Williams wrote, "let us not sell it cheap."[18]

What the principle means is that we have a responsibility to be right, but with modesty; for we, too, may be wrong. Arrogance is not the claim to be right, but the refusal to admit even the possibility that we might be wrong. ("We have received from Divine Providence," the Emperor Constantine declared immodestly, "the supreme favor of being relieved from all error."[19])

Second, respect for freedom of conscience means that, while we respect people's right to believe what their conscience dictates that they believe, even if we think they are dead wrong, we have a right and sometimes a duty to disagree with them, though their right to believe has to be countered by our responsibility to disagree with them civilly and persuasively.

Tolerance is infinitely better than its opposite: intolerance. But tolerance that is blasé about error and evil, and tolerance that flip-flops into intolerance, are two sides of the same bad coin. Equally, it is bad to be silenced and not allowed to speak, but it is no better to be seduced by polite words and a politically correct atmosphere. Far better to have a tough-minded view of tolerance that simultaneously knows what it believes and respects the right of others to their beliefs, and knows how to debate forcefully but civilly when there is disagreement.

This right to be wrong can be defended from two perspectives. One is the standpoint of reason. Montaigne, for example, said of the "sharp, vigorous exchanges" that he liked: "It is not strong enough nor magnanimous enough if it is not argumentative, if all is politeness and art; if it is afraid of clashes and walks hobbled: '*Necque enim disputari sine reprehensione potest*' [It is impossible to debate without refuting]."[20]

But the right to be wrong has also been defended stoutly from the standpoint of faith. In his great attack on censorship in *Areopagitica*, John Milton drew on a biblical understanding of the intertwining of good and evil, wheat and tares. There is always the danger that in trying to uproot the false and the bad, we also destroy the true and the good. He therefore defended the right to be wrong, and disparaged "a fugitive and cloistered virtue, unexercised and unbreathed." The better way was "a trial by what is contrary," because "our faith and knowledge thrives by exercise, as well as our limbs and complexion."[21] Similarly, John Wesley urged his followers, religious liberty did not mean that they did not have strong beliefs or that having strong beliefs meant that they imposed them on others, but rather that "they think and let think."[22]

A Global Public Square

Those who would still dismiss the notion of an American civil public square as empty idealism should consider two further points. *First, the search for a civil public square in America is made all the more urgent by the emergence of a global square.* Just as sound carries across water, so discussion and debate in a global era now almost instantly become a global conversation. Witness the worldwide Muslim response to Salman Rushdie's *Satanic Verses*, to Jerry Falwell's remarks about the prophet Muhammad, to the Danish cartoons, or to the pope's speech: "Rude remarks in Lynchburg, riots in Lahore."

Thanks to the wonders of technology, such a global public square is beginning to emerge, and it raises the same issues as the American public square with a vengeance. Living with our deepest differences is all the more difficult because of the increased intensity of global diversity, global conflict, and the lack of any constructive global precedents for civility. But curiously, the same three tendencies that are at work in the United States are starting to show their face in the emerging global square, so it is urgent for farsighted leaders to articulate and demonstrate the vision that is best, and to do so before the mold begins to set and harden.

On one side in the global public square are the advocates of various visions of *progressive universalism*—those who believe that their way is the only way and the one way for everyone, and who are prepared to coerce others into believing their way, too. Among those in this category are not only obvious groups such as communists and Islamists, but less obvious groups such as a motley array of liberals, feminists, democrats, capitalists, and globalists, all of whom are eager to carry their message to the world, and (at least in their opponents' eyes) to promote it with force if necessary. In short, in good Enlightenment fashion, progress in the Western way is made the universal future for all humankind ("the West is best").

William Pitt the Younger's warning about revolutionary France in 1792 would apply to many global-era movements and also to apprehensions about the universal pretensions of the United States: "Unless she is stopped in her career, all Europe must soon learn their ideas of justice—law of nations—models of government—and principles of liberty from the mouth of French cannon."[23]

In a world as diverse and divided as ours, in which there are properly many different ways to be modern, the outcome of this first approach to the global public square is plain: *conflict* and increased hostility.

On the other side are advocates of a vision of *multicultural relativism*—those who believe that nations as much as individuals are free to believe, and to live as they choose to believe, and that it is no business of anyone else's to interfere in that freedom. Coming as we do from widely different faiths, worldviews, and cultural backgrounds, who are any of us to judge anyone else? It all depends on how each of us sees it, and no one has the right to judge anyone else, or to interfere in anyone else's life.

For example, in 1947 the executive board of the American Anthropological Association refused to sign the United Nations Declaration of Universal Human Rights on the grounds that it was an "ethnocentric document." After all, as anthropologists know, human rights are Western in origin and far from universal. Failure to see this is "First World conceit" and becomes an easy justification for the "imperialism" of the "new evangelists" of the Western style of progress.

Far more humane and tolerant at first sight, this vision is also inadequate. For if the progressive universalist vision leads directly to *conflict,* the multicultural relativist vision leads directly to *complacency*—toward evil and human oppression. If everything is a matter of cultural relativism and none of us has the right to judge another, was Bartolomé de Las Casas wrong to stand against the conquistadores, or William Wilberforce to fight for the abolition of slavery, or Martin Luther King Jr. to resist Jim Crow laws, or Simon Wiesenthal to track down Nazi criminals, or feminists to fight against the mutilation of female genitalia today?

To be sure, the moral duty to intervene at times means that there must be clear moral and political guidelines to distinguish between legitimate and illegitimate "interference." But in an age of violence to women, globalized crime, terrorism, human trafficking, and genocide, a failure to make judgments and a failure to intervene are not a sign of being humane but of a deep deficiency of humanity and a reverse imperialism that would freeze cultures in time and leave the poor and the oppressed to their plight.

The third option for the global public square is a vision of *civility* through *covenant pluralism:* everyone in the world is free to believe what they choose to believe, on the basis of freedom of conscience; but, as with the civil public square, they have to accord the same freedom to others, and learn to live with a double eye—one to the integrity of their own faiths, and the other to the responsibility of seeing and dealing with others through the lens of their faiths. In short, recognizing and respecting the difference of others, without relinquishing the integrity of one's own faith, is a prerequisite for global freedom and justice.

The third position confronts American Christians, and especially Christians in the Religious Right, with a clear choice. In the eyes of many, American Christians are associated with the first option—progressive universalism, and the imposition of one way on everyone—which is why Christians appear so threatening to so many.

On the one hand, the Christian faith is the world's first truly global faith, the world's largest faith, and the world's most diverse community. It offers the world's most translated and translatable scriptures, and in many parts of the world it is the fastest-growing faith. On the other hand, the Christian church over the centuries has carried its universal message in two entirely contradictory ways—the way of Jesus of Nazareth and the way of the Roman emperor Constantine.

Both ways have been universal in their message, though in quite different ways. The way of Jesus was the way of a servant, aiming to bring justice and peace to the world, emptying himself of legitimate power, and being prepared to suffer and die in carrying out his task. The way of Constantine, on the other hand, was the way of a conqueror able to impose his will on the world despite all resistance. What would be disastrous at this early stage of the global public square would be a combination of attitudes created by American superpower strength, Constantinian Christian attitudes, and an overheated, apocalyptic, end-times fundamentalist style of thinking. Christians must choose and follow the way of Jesus rather then the way of Contantine.

Beware Two-Tier Tolerance

Many Americans now suspect that the prospects for a rich, mature civility are too challenging even in their own public square, inspite of all their rich American heritage of principles, pitfalls, and lessons. Not surprisingly, civility in the global public square seems even more unlikely, if not utopian. This is why neglect and resignation are likely to cause a slow slide toward an unsatisfactory compromise that is a travesty of equality of freedom of conscience for all: the emergence of a two-tier global public square.

The top tier, needless to say, will be occupied by the global elites that see themselves as broadly cosmopolitan, liberal, and secular. The second tier will be peopled by those who make up the bulk of the world, whose religious beliefs will be particular to their local area, and who will be tolerated so long as their faith remains private and inoffensive. At best, the two-tier view would be a return to tolerance as condescension; at worst it would be a cover for "totalitolerance" as coercion and a denial of free exercise.

The likely shape of the global public square is still out of sight, but the interests of freedom and justice are plain even at this early stage of its formation. Which raises in turn the second imperative to make Americans work toward restoring civility in their own public square now. The most realistic prompter to such needed change is not idealism but crisis.

At one level, global problems such as the risks of nuclear terrorism, bird flu, climate change, scarce resources, and genetically modified foods have become the stuff of watercooler conversations. But at another level, problems such as a global public square remain abstract for most people. September 11 should have changed all that, and shown the limitations of nation-states and the futility of the quest for total security; and shown, too, that in a dangerously divided world, force of arms cannot be the normal language for conversation among the peoples of the earth.

Down that road lies the terrible prospect that Neitzsche foresaw: of "great politics" and "a war of spirits," the likes of which "have never yet been on earth."[24] In sum, the global crises are showing us that a cosmopolitan and civil public square, whether in America today or around the world at some future date, is far from utopian; it is an immediate priority. The art of living with our deepest differences is not a luxury topic for philosophers or futurists, but an urgent matter for everyone concerned with civilized life and human survival. Civility is a key not only to civil society but to civilization itself.

Chapter Seven

Starting with Ourselves

In early 1999, as the U.S. Senate was considering the impeachment of President Clinton, I happened to have a series of breakfasts and lunches over the course of two weeks with some of the best-known journalists and opinion shapers in Washington, D.C. At the end of my conversation with the first one, I asked him almost casually who spoke for him at the national level. More specifically:

"Which national leader do you think has the vision, the character, the courage, the grasp of history, the understanding of America and the world, and of course the access to a camera and a microphone, to speak as a statesman in this time of national crisis?"

He thought for a moment, and then said simply, "No one. I can think of someone who would have done it ten years ago, but he's too close to retirement to risk it now. But today? No one. There is no one who speaks for me like that."

I was so struck by his answer that I made a point of asking each of the people I met with. Not a single one said anyone.

Since then, I have put the question to scores of people in different parts of the country, and their answers often set off a searching discussion on the need for such statesmen today, and why there are so few.

Reasons for the apparent dearth of leadership have been much discussed: from the dismissal of character in leadership, to the shift to management at the expense of leadership, to the loss of history in education, to the weakening of the aggregating role of the parties and the opening up of political candidacy to the ambitious and the wealthy, to the rise of a celebrity culture, and so on.

The outcome is sobering. Two and a third centuries after the audacious work of the brilliant generation that comprised the founding fathers, with all the changes and developments that have occurred since then, a full range of questions is pressing for America's attention. These questions call for a leader of the stature of the founders—or Abraham Lincoln or Franklin Roosevelt—to wrestle with them and address them in order to point the way to a new, new birth of freedom.

So far no such a leader has emerged, and some would argue that it is not likely that such a leader will emerge. The constitutionally required annual State of the Union Address, for example, often slips into a self-congratulatory media event, a political celebration of each passing incumbent of 1600 Pennsylvania Avenue, and a series of soaring sermons on America's ideals. As such, the leading role requires only a politician, not a statesman. More important, there is a dearth of statesmen, leaders with sufficient character, sense of history, deep grasp of the American experiment, moral courage, vision of the future, and the access to a camera and microphone, to stand alone without aides, speechwriters, and spin doctors and address the real state of the union.

Great leaders, it is said, are always thrown up in great crises. But it would be more accurate to say that a nation's health can always be gauged by its capacity to produce such a leader in its hour of crisis—what Lincoln was in the Civil War, what Roosevelt was during the Depression, and what Churchill was in World War II. Yet if this is true, the United States is waiting for such a leader today, and nowhere is the need more urgent than over the issue at hand.

What Is to Be Done?

Such thinking is correct and important, but it conceals a trap. It lets us off the hook, and plays into the hands of elitism and citizen passivity. What would it take to stand against the extremes of the culture wars, to restore a cosmopolitan and civil public square, to work toward what might be a new, new birth of freedom in our time, and to provide a model for the world on how to live with our deepest differences? There are things that only leaders can do, but the real restoration must begin with us. A full discussion of the practical steps needed is beyond the scope of this book, though I would mention the barest outline here.

First, it is plain beyond doubt what must not be done.

Continuing the present course of the culture wars spells disaster for the United States and a historic failure to seize the moment and demonstrate to the world the significance of the American experiment. Equally, it would be folly to presume that the country is merely experiencing another swing of the pendulum, or that it will simply muddle through somehow, or that this is just the latest of America's periodic surprised discoveries by journalists and commentators of "how extraordinarily religious the American people are," or that "things are really not that bad because the election of 1800 was worse," or even that despite everything, according to the old adage, "God will always take care of babies, drunks, and the United States." Against all such characteristically American kinds of drift and complacency, it must be said firmly: The facts are on the table, the stakes are high, and the moment of opportunity is closing. Unless the present generation restores civility in public life, the American republic will decline.

Second, restoring sustainable freedom means starting with ourselves.

This is no moment to wait for others and above all to wait for some great leader. All who live in this country, along with the citizens of all the world's democracies, are the beneficiaries of this great heritage of ordered freedom, or "federal liberty." We are each the living links between our parents and our children, and it is our task to keep the precious flame alive. We each have the freedom to speak and act in our open society. We are each citizens who are primary stakeholders in our worlds. We each have spheres of influence in which our voices can be heard and in which our authority counts. We are each the ones whose power to choose determines the quality of our community and public life in a thousand small but vital ways.

It is therefore up to each of us to think long and hard about the present state of things, to consider the outcome of current attitudes, to challenge the grip of dominant ways of thinking, to model the civility and persuasion we should like to see in public life, to switch off programs or unsubscribe to magazines that further the problem, to stop voting for leaders or donating to political parties and organizations whose short-term tactics undermine the long-term good, to demand a leadership worthy of America and its world responsibility at this hour, and to determine that destructive incivility may flourish, "but not through me."

The fact is that culture warring will not preserve American freedom any more than lies will foster truth and litigiousness will guarantee rights. But if we would like a society of truth, freedom, justice, and decency, we must be people of truth, freedom, justice, and decency. If we would like our views and our deeply held faiths to be understood and respected by those who differ from with us, we must understand and show respect to them and theirs. If we would like to be treated decently and fairly, we must be decent and fair to others. If we would engage with rational and fair arguments from others, we must argue rationally and fairly ourselves. If we would like others not to be taken in by lies and falsehoods spread about us, we must not fall for lies and falsehoods spread about others.

Most especially, if we are either liberal or conservative, we must be vigilant to see that we ourselves are liberal in our free and generous attitudes toward conservatives, or conservative in maintaining the great traditions of past civility in our attitudes toward liberals. If we wish civility to be a robust and freely chosen virtue, we ourselves must be dedicated to it as a covenant rather than a contract, as a matter of justice as much as power, and as a life-giving habit of the heart rather than a dead and deadening letter of any law.

Above all, we must not only decry the darkness but spread the light. We must not only protest the letter of the First Amendment but live the spirit of its principles—people of conscience in our faiths, who respect the right of freedom of conscience for others; people of truth in our speech, who recognize the right of others to speak freely, too; and people of love in our communities, who recognizing the right of freedom of assembly for all, including those whose same freedom of conscience leads them to speak and assemble in order to disagree with us.

In sum, the responsibility for restoring a civil and cosmopolitan public square does not rest solely with the White House, Capitol Hill, the television network president, the newspaper owner, the company boss, the school principal, or the grassroots activist leader. It begins and ends with us.

Third, restoring sustainable freedom requires a resolute assertion of leadership.

Too much American leadership today is an other-directed form of pandering, with politicians and others forever sniffing the polling winds and anxiously reading focus-group tea leaves. For this reason alone, it can be said that America has the leadership it deserves. At the same time, courageous leaders who are prepared to stand for what is right and wise rather than popular always need support and affirmation— and votes. "Starting with us" therefore means demanding a quality of leadership that matches the moment we face.

The present hour requires from America a national leader and statesman—not a mere politician, not a manager, not a celebrity, not a demagogue, not a figurehead, but a statesman with a deep grasp of the American experiment, an expansive understanding of American history, a wise experience of the contours of the modern global world, an indomitable courage to stand against powerful political forces, and the ability to speak with such vision and power that new vistas are opened for the American people to see and head toward.

Other levels of leadership are needed, too—from other politicians, television anchors, university presidents, religious leaders, journalists, activists, school-board members, and local leaders who are prepared to break with present patterns and conduct the nation's affairs in a manner worthy of a republic. Such efforts are important in their own right, but on their own they would not amount to what is required unless a truly national leader speaks, acts, and organizes in a way that opens a new path through the battle-scarred terrain of the culture wars.

Fourth, restoring the civil public square requires a remarkable articulation of vision.

Two and a third centuries after the American Revolution, with a deep awareness of the changing conditions of history and a realistic eye to the mounting challenges of global leadership in the global era, an American leader needs to set out an American vision for today—as true to the stunning achievements of the American past as to the staggering challenges of the world's future.

This is no moment for the shortsighted or for those uncomfortable with "the vision thing." Only a vision of a free, civil, cosmopolitan America in a free, civil, cosmopolitan world can stir American hearts and minds and recapture the imagination of an increasingly suspicious and resentful world.

Such a vision must be global in its appeal yet modest in its pretensions, all-American rather than partisan, and neither narrowly conservative nor thoughtlessly liberal. It must span the world of the past as easily as the world of today and tomorrow. It must challenge and win the advocates of a sacred public square, but satisfy the legitimate concerns behind their stands; and challenge and win the advocates of a naked public square while recognizing their important new considerations that the founders did not have to take into account. The courage required to conceive such a vision would be matched only by the courage required to deliver it.

Fifth, restoring the civil public square requires a realistic application of the vision and its principles to the leading trouble spots in the culture wars.

Of the making of the present flashpoints in the culture wars there is no end. But unquestionably, the two main storm centers of controversy today are the public square itself—which now includes the burgeoning, often irrational, and highly manipulative Web logs—and public education, the schoolhouse being the microcosm and the seedbed of the public square, just as the Muslim madrasas are the seedbed of both the strife and the hope for reformation within Islam today.

Will election campaigns once again involve serious debate over serious issues, as the times demand? Will news programs expand beyond the sound-bite format, the entertainment style, and the parochial American focus, as world responsibility requires? Will activist organizations come to write direct-mail letters whose powerful arguments do not need to rely on hate and fear? Will genuine debating surmount the emotional venting on the blogs? Will a restored civility allow public schools once again to cultivate the habits of the heart among six-year-olds, twelve-year-olds, and eighteen-year-olds who can take their place as citizens and leaders in a civil America of tomorrow?

Questions such as these point to the need for highly practical solutions in a hundred areas, but the promise is as great as the peril. Restore civility in the public square and the public school, and sustain it from generation to generation, and it would spread throughout the nation, renew the wellsprings of the republic, and change the course of history. (Both spheres require a bold, patient, and highly practical and systematic application of the principles of civility—within the framework of a vision such as the Williamsburg Charter and along the lines of the patient and effective but unheralded initiatives of the Common Ground movement led by Charles Haynes, Oliver Thomas, and other doughty champions of religious liberty.[1]) Fail to do so, on the other hand, and America's days of greatness are numbered.

Message in a Bottle?

To many people, the thought of standing against the culture wars and of reforging a cosmopolitan and civil public square seems a thankless if not forlorn task. In candid moments, people tell me it would be like spitting against the wind, or casting out a message in a bottle onto the stormy seas of American public life. Will the message survive the storms? Will it be picked up on some far shore and read by some unknown rescuer who will not only pay attention but understand the message; and not only understand but act, and act in time?

People often use the picture of a message in a bottle to illustrate the countless obstacles, unknowns, and ironies of communicating in the age of communication. At best, the image of the bottle cast upon the waters rises above the level of a futile, despairing gesture only on the strength of two assumptions: the belief that the message is worth launching, and the belief that the message is worth the finder's time to pick up and respond to.

I understand when people use that image to express to me the daunting challenges, but the image is far too weak to express my own confidence and hope. Certainly, America's underlying problems are often more serious and lie elsewhere than many Americans realize, but the great American adventure need not be over, and the way forward can begin with a resolute reexamination and renewal of the sources of American greatness.

Yet the task will not be easy. When I worked on drafting the Williamsburg Charter and building the coalition of support, I used to remind myself of Henrik Ibsen's homespun advice: "One should never put on one's best trousers to go out to battle for freedom and truth."[2] There were several months when I received a series of letters containing death threats from what must truly be the far, Far Right, though I would have to say that I was equally troubled by the day-to-day duplicity and malice of some of the Left who purported to be liberal but whose behavior was despicable.

I have no illusions about the challenges involved and the sacrifices required.

Recently, many domestic and international American policies have been, to put the point charitably, less than fully successful and less than worthy of the American promise. One of their legacies is an acrid bitterness in public life that affects all positive proposals, making the constructive seem idealistic, the difficult impossible, and the visionary utopian. Yet we must never forget that the present course of the culture wars also spells decline for America.

At the same time, a resurgent groundswell of public support, a reassertion of leadership, a reforging of a cosmopolitan and civil public square, and a reapplication of the fruits of such initiatives in areas such as public-policy debates and public education could even be the key to yet another renewal of freedom—which in turn would be a vital part of America's becoming a world power worthy of free people, and so living up to its astonishing birthright of freedom.

Living with our deepest differences is one of the world's great issues. Does history's "new order of the ages" still have within itself the capacity to declare and demonstrate an answer, and help make a world safe for diversity? Or has America reached the outer limits of what is possible within the framework of the American experiment, so that her resources are stretched too thin to answer the challenge? The world awaits America's answer.

Afterword

THE WILLIAMSBURG CHARTER

*A Celebration and Reaffirmation
of the First Amendment*

Introduction

Keenly aware of the high national purpose of commemorating the bicentennial of the United States Constitution, we who sign this Charter seek to celebrate the Constitution's greatness, and to call for a bold reaffirmation and reappraisal of its vision and guiding principles. In particular, we call for a fresh consideration of religious liberty in our time, and of the place of the First Amendment Religious Liberty clauses in our national life.

We gratefully acknowledge that the Constitution has been hailed as America's "chief export" and "the most wonderful work ever struck off at a given time by the brain and purpose of man." Today, two hundred years after its signing, the Constitution is not only the world's oldest, still-effective written constitution, but the admired pattern of ordered liberty for countless people in many lands.

In spite of its enduring and universal qualities, however, some provisions of the Constitution are now the subject of widespread controversy in the United States. One area of intense controversy concerns the First Amendment Religious Liberty clauses, whose mutually reinforcing provisions act as a double guarantee of religious liberty, one part barring the making of any law "respecting an establishment of religion" and the other barring any law "prohibiting the free exercise thereof."

The First Amendment Religious Liberty provisions epitomize the Constitution's visionary realism. They were, as James Madison said, the "true remedy" to the predicament of religious conflict they originally addressed, and they well express the responsibilities and limits of the state with respect to liberty and justice.

Our commemoration of the Constitution's bicentennial must therefore go beyond celebration to rededication. Unless this is done, an irreplaceable part of national life will be endangered, and a remarkable opportunity for the expansion of liberty will be lost.

For we judge that the present controversies over religion in public life pose both a danger and an opportunity. There is evident danger in the fact that certain forms of politically reassertive religion in parts of the world are, in principle, enemies of democratic freedom and a source of deep social antagonism. There is also evident opportunity in the growing philosophical and cultural awareness that all people live by commitments and ideals, that value-neutrality is impossible in the ordering of society, and that we are on the edge of a promising moment for a fresh assessment of pluralism and liberty. It is with an eye to both the promise and the peril that we publish this Charter and pledge ourselves to its principles.

We readily acknowledge our continuing differences. Signing this Charter implies no pretense that we believe the same things or that our differences over policy proposals, legal interpretations and philosophical groundings do not ultimately matter. The truth is not even that what unites us is deeper than what divides us, for differences over belief are the deepest and least easily negotiated of all.

The Charter sets forth a renewed national compact, in the sense of a solemn mutual agreement between parties, on how we view the place of religion in American life and how we should contend with each other's deepest differences in the public sphere. It is a call to a vision of public life that will allow conflict to lead to consensus, religious commitment to reinforce political civility. In this way, diversity is not a point of weakness but a source of strength.

A Time for Reaffirmation

We believe, in the first place, that the nature of the Religious Liberty clauses must be understood before the problems surrounding them can be resolved. We therefore affirm both their cardinal assumptions and the reasons for their crucial national importance.

With regard to the assumptions of the First Amendment Religious Liberty clauses, we hold three to be chief:

The Inalienable Right

Nothing is more characteristic of humankind than the natural and inescapable drive toward meaning and belonging, toward making sense of life and finding community in the world. As fundamental and precious as life itself, this "will to meaning" finds expression in ultimate beliefs, whether theistic or non-theistic, transcendent or naturalistic, and these beliefs are most our own when a matter of conviction rather than coercion. They are most our own when, in the words of George Mason, the principal author of the Virginia Declaration of Rights, they are "directed only by reason and conviction, not by force or violence."

As James Madison expressed it in his Memorial and Remonstrance, "The Religion then of every man must be left to the conviction and conscience of every man; and it is the right of every man to exercise it as these may dictate. This right is in its nature an unalienable right."

Two hundred years later, despite dramatic changes in life and a marked increase of naturalistic philosophies in some parts of the world and in certain sectors of our society, this right to religious liberty based upon freedom of conscience remains fundamental and inalienable. While particular beliefs may be true or false, better or worse, the right to reach, hold, exercise them freely, or change them, is basic and non-negotiable.

Religious liberty finally depends on neither the favors of the state and its officials nor the vagaries of tyrants or majorities. Religious liberty in a democracy is a right that may not be submitted to vote and depends on the outcome of no election. A society is only as just and free as it is respectful of this right, especially toward the beliefs of its smallest minorities and least popular communities.

The right to freedom of conscience is premised not upon science, nor upon social utility, nor upon pride of species. Rather, it is premised upon the inviolable dignity of the human person. It is the foundation of, and is integrally related to, all other rights and freedoms secured by the Constitution. This basic civil liberty is clearly acknowledged in the Declaration of Independence and is ineradicable from the long tradition of rights and liberties from which the Revolution sprang.

The Ever Present Danger

No threat to freedom of conscience and religious liberty has historically been greater than the coercions of both Church and State. These two institutions—the one religious, the other political—have through the centuries succumbed to the temptation of coercion in their claims over minds and souls. When these institutions and their claims have been combined, it has too often resulted in terrible violations of human liberty and dignity. They are so combined when the sword and purse of the State are in the hands of the Church, or when the State usurps the mantle of the Church so as to coerce the conscience and compel belief. These and other such confusions of religion and state authority represent the misordering of religion and government which it is the purpose of the Religious Liberty provisions to prevent.

Authorities and orthodoxies have changed, kingdoms and empires have come and gone, yet as John Milton once warned, "new Presbyter is but old priest writ large." Similarly, the modern persecutor of religion is but ancient tyrant with more refined instruments of control. Moreover, many of the greatest crimes against conscience of this century have been committed, not by religious authorities, but by ideologues virulently opposed to traditional religion.

Yet whether ancient or modern, issuing from religion or ideology, the result is the same: religious and ideological orthodoxies, when politically established, lead only too naturally toward what Roger Williams called a "spiritual rape" that coerces the conscience and produces "rivers of civil blood" that stain the record of human history.

Less dramatic but also lethal to freedom and the chief menace to religious liberty today is the expanding power of government control over personal behavior and the institutions of society, when the government acts not so much in deliberate hostility to, but in reckless disregard of, communal belief and personal conscience.

Thanks principally to the wisdom of the First Amendment, the American experience is different. But even in America where state-established orthodoxies are unlawful and the state is constitutionally limited, religious liberty can never be taken for granted. It is a rare achievement that requires constant protection.

The Most Nearly Perfect Solution

Knowing well that "nothing human can be perfect" (James Madison) and that the Constitution was not "a faultless work" (Gouverneur Morris), the Framers nevertheless saw the First Amendment as a "true remedy" and the most nearly perfect solution yet devised for properly ordering the relationship of religion and the state in a free society.

There have been occasions when the protections of the First Amendment have been overridden or imperfectly applied. Nonetheless, the First Amendment is a momentous decision for religious liberty, the most important political decision for religious liberty and public justice in the history of humankind. Limitation upon religious liberty is allowable only where the State has borne a heavy burden of proof that the limitation is justified—not by any ordinary public interest, but by a supreme public necessity—and that no less restrictive alternative to limitation exists.

The Religious Liberty clauses are a brilliant construct in which both No establishment and Free exercise serve the ends of religious liberty and freedom of conscience. No longer can sword, purse and sacred mantle be equated. Now, the government is barred from using religion's mantle to become a confessional State, and from allowing religion to use the government's sword and purse to become a coercing Church. In this new order, the freedom of the government from religious control and the freedom of religion from government control are a double guarantee of the protection of rights. No faith is preferred or prohibited, for where there is no state-definable orthodoxy, there can be no state-punishable heresy.

With regard to the reasons why the First Amendment Religious Liberty clauses are important for the nation today, we hold five to be pre-eminent:

The First Amendment Religious Liberty provisions have both a logical and historical priority in the Bill of Rights. They have logical priority because the security of all rights rests upon the recognition that they are neither given by the state, nor can they be taken away by the state. Such rights are inherent in the inviolability of the human person. History demonstrates that unless these rights are protected our society's slow, painful progress toward freedom would not have been possible.

The First Amendment Religious Liberty provisions lie close to the heart of the distinctiveness of the American

experiment. The uniqueness of the American way of disestablishment and its consequences have often been more
obvious to foreign observers such as Alexis de Tocqueville
and Lord James Bryce, who wrote that "of all the differences between the Old world and the New, this is perhaps the most salient." In particular, the Religious Liberty
clauses are vital to harnessing otherwise centrifugal forces
such as personal liberty and social diversity, thus sustaining republican vitality while making possible a necessary
measure of national concord.

The First Amendment Religious Liberty provisions are
the democratic world's most salient alternative to the totalitarian repression of human rights and provide a cor-
rective to unbridled nationalism and religious warfare
around the world.

The First Amendment Religious Liberty provisions provide the United States' most distinctive answer to one of
the world's most pressing questions in the late-twentieth
century. They address the problem: How do we live with
each other's deepest differences? How do religious convictions and political freedom complement rather than
threaten each other on a small planet in a pluralistic age?
In a world in which bigotry, fanaticism, terrorism and the
state control of religion are all too common responses to
these questions, sustaining the justice and liberty of the
American arrangement is an urgent moral task.

The First Amendment Religious Liberty provisions
give American society a unique position in relation to
both the First and Third worlds. Highly modernized
like the rest of the First World, yet not so secularized,
this society—largely because of religious freedom—
remains, like most of the Third World, deeply religious.
This fact, which is critical for possibilities of better
human understanding, has not been sufficiently appreciated in American self-understanding, or drawn upon
in American diplomacy and communication throughout the world.

In sum, as much if not more than any other single provision in the entire Constitution, the Religious Liberty provisions hold the key to American distinctiveness and American destiny. Far from being settled by the interpretations of judges and historians, the last word on the First Amendment likely rests in a chapter yet to be written, documenting the unfolding drama of America. If religious liberty is neglected, all civil liberties will suffer. If it is guarded and sustained, the American experiment will be the more secure.

A Time for Reappraisal

Much of the current controversy about religion and politics neither reflects the highest wisdom of the First Amendment nor serves the best interests of the disputants or the nation. We therefore call for a critical reappraisal of the course and consequences of such controversy. Four widespread errors have exacerbated the controversy needlessly.

The Issue Is Not Only What We Debate, but How

The debate about religion in public life is too often misconstrued as a clash of ideologies alone, pitting "secularists" against the "sectarians" or vice versa. Though competing and even contrary worldviews are involved, the controversy is not solely ideological. It also flows from a breakdown in understanding of how personal and communal beliefs should be related to public life.

The American republic depends upon the answers to two questions. By what ultimate truths ought we to live? And how should these be related to public life? The first question is personal, but has a public dimension because of the connection between beliefs and public virtue. The American answer to the first question is that the government is excluded from giving an answer. The second question, however, is thoroughly public in character, and a public answer is appropriate and necessary to the well-being of this society.

This second question was central to the idea of the First Amendment. The Religious Liberty provisions are not "articles of faith" concerned with the substance of particular doctrines or of policy issues. They are "articles of peace" concerned with the constitutional constraints and the shared prior understanding within which the American people can engage their differences in a civil manner and thus provide for both religious liberty and stable public government.

Conflicts over the relationship between deeply held beliefs and public policy will remain a continuing feature of democratic life. They do not discredit the First Amendment, but confirm its wisdom and point to the need to distinguish the Religious Liberty clauses from the particular controversies they address. The clauses can never be divorced from the controversies they address, but should always be held distinct. In the public discussion, an open commitment to the constraints and standards of the clauses should precede and accompany debate over the controversies.

The Issue Is Not Sectarian, but National

The role of religion in American public life is too often devalued or dismissed in public debate, as though the American people's historically vital religious traditions were at best a purely private matter and at worst essentially sectarian and divisive.

Such a position betrays a failure of civil respect for the convictions of others. It also underestimates the degree to which the Framers relied on the American people's religious convictions to be what Tocqueville described as "the first of their political institutions." In America, this crucial public role has been played by diverse beliefs, not so much despite disestablishment as because of disestablishment.

The Founders knew well that the republic they established represented an audacious gamble against long historical odds. This form of government depends upon ultimate beliefs, for otherwise we have no right to the rights by which it thrives, yet rejects any official formulation of them. The republic will therefore always remain an "undecided experiment" that stands or falls by the dynamism of its non-established faiths.

The Issue Is Larger Than the Disputants

Recent controversies over religion and public life have too often become a form of warfare in which individuals, motives and reputations have been impugned. The intensity of the debate is commensurate with the importance of the issues debated, but to those engaged in this warfare we present two arguments for reappraisal and restraint.

The lesser argument is one of expediency and is based on the ironic fact that each side has become the best argument for the other. One side's excesses have become the other side's arguments; one side's extremists the other side's recruiters. The danger is that, as the ideological warfare becomes self-perpetuating, more serious issues and broader national interests will be forgotten and the bitterness deepened.

The more important argument is one of principle and is based on the fact that the several sides have pursued their objectives in ways which contradict their own best ideals. Too often, for example, religious believers have been uncharitable, liberals have been illiberal, conservatives have been insensitive to tradition, champions of tolerance have been intolerant, defenders of free speech have been censorious, and citizens of a republic based on democratic accommodation have succumbed to a habit of relentless confrontation.

The Issue Is Understandably Threatening

The First Amendment's meaning is too often debated in ways that ignore the genuine grievances or justifiable fears of opposing points of view. This happens when the logic of opposing arguments favors either an unwarranted intrusion of religion into public life or an unwarranted exclusion of religion from it. History plainly shows that with religious control over government, political freedom dies; with political control over religion, religious freedom dies.

The First Amendment has contributed to avoiding both these perils, but this happy experience is no cause for complacency. Though the United States has escaped the worst excesses experienced elsewhere in the world, the republic has shown two distinct tendencies of its own, one in the past and one today.

In earlier times, though lasting well into the twentieth century, there was a de facto semi-establishment of one religion in the United States: a generalized Protestantism given dominant status in national institutions, especially in the public schools. This development was largely approved by Protestants, but widely opposed by non-Protestants, including Catholics and Jews.

In more recent times, and partly in reaction, constitutional jurisprudence has tended, in the view of many, to move toward the de facto semi-establishment of a wholly secular understanding of the origin, nature and destiny of humankind and of the American nation. During this period, the exclusion of teaching about the role of religion in society, based partly upon a misunderstanding of First Amendment decisions, has ironically resulted in giving a dominant status to such wholly secular understandings in many national institutions. Many secularists appear as unconcerned over the consequences of this development as were Protestants unconcerned about their de facto establishment earlier.

Such de facto establishments, though seldom extreme, usually benign and often unwitting, are the source of grievances and fears among the several parties in current controversies. Together with the encroachments of the expanding modern state, such de facto establishments, as much as any official establishment, are likely to remain a threat to freedom and justice for all.

Justifiable fears are raised by those who advocate theocracy or the coercive power of law to establish a "Christian America." While this advocacy is and should be legally protected, such proposals contradict freedom of conscience and the genius of the Religious Liberty provisions.

At the same time there are others who raise justifiable fears of an unwarranted exclusion of religion from public life. The assertion of moral judgments as though they were morally neutral, and interpretations of the "wall of separation" that would exclude religious expression and argument from public life, also contradict freedom of conscience and the genius of the provisions.

Civility obliges citizens in a pluralistic society to take great care in using words and casting issues. The communications media have a primary role, and thus a special responsibility, in shaping public opinion and debate. Words such as public, secular and religious should be free from discriminatory bias. "Secular purpose," for example, should not mean "non-religious purpose" but "general public purpose." Otherwise, the impression is gained that "public is equivalent to secular; religion is equivalent to private." Such equations are neither accurate nor just. Similarly, it is false to equate "public" and "governmental." In a society that sets store by the necessary limits on government, there are many spheres of life that are public but non-governmental.

Two important conclusions follow from a reappraisal of the present controversies over religion in public life. First, the process of adjustment and readjustment to the constraints and standards of the Religious Liberty provisions is an ongoing requirement of American democracy. The Constitution is not a self-interpreting, self-executing document; and the prescriptions of the Religious Liberty provisions cannot by themselves resolve the myriad confusions and ambiguities surrounding the right ordering of the relationship between religion and government in a free society. The Framers clearly understood that the Religious Liberty provisions provide the legal construct for what must be an ongoing process of adjustment and mutual give-and-take in a democracy.

We are keenly aware that, especially over state-supported education, we as a people must continue to wrestle with the complex connections between religion and the transmission of moral values in a pluralistic society. Thus, we cannot have, and should not seek, a definitive, once for all solution to the questions that will continue to surround the Religious Liberty provisions.

Second, the need for such a readjustment today can best be addressed by remembering that the two clauses are essentially one provision for preserving religious liberty. Both parts, No establishment and Free exercise, are to be comprehensively understood as being in the service of religious liberty as a positive good. At the heart of the Establishment clause is the prohibition of state sponsorship of religion and at the heart of Free exercise clause is the prohibition of state interference with religious liberty.

No sponsorship means that the state must leave to the free citizenry the public expression of ultimate beliefs, religious or otherwise, providing only that no expression is excluded from, and none governmentally favored, in the continuing democratic discourse.

No interference means the assurance of voluntary religious expression free from governmental intervention. This includes placing religious expression on an equal footing with all other forms of expression in genuinely public forums.

No sponsorship and no interference together mean fair opportunity. That is to say, all faiths are free to enter vigorously into public life and to exercise such influence as their followers and ideas engender. Such democratic exercise of influence is in the best tradition of American voluntarism and is not an unwarranted "imposition" or "establishment."

A Time for Reconstitution

We believe, finally, that the time is ripe for a genuine expansion of democratic liberty, and that this goal may be attained through a new engagement of citizens in a debate that is reordered in accord with constitutional first principles and considerations of the common good. This amounts to no less than the reconstitution of a free republican people in our day. Careful consideration of three precepts would advance this possibility:

The Criteria Must Be Multiple

Reconstitution requires the recognition that the great dangers in interpreting the Constitution today are either to release interpretation from any demanding criteria or to narrow the criteria excessively. The first relaxes the necessary restraining force of the Constitution, while the second overlooks the insights that have arisen from the Constitution in two centuries of national experience.

Religious liberty is the only freedom in the First Amendment to be given two provisions. Together the clauses form a strong bulwark against suppression of religious liberty, yet they emerge from a series of dynamic tensions which cannot ultimately be relaxed. The Religious Liberty provisions grow out of an understanding not only of rights and a due recognition of faiths but of realism and a due recognition of factions. They themselves reflect both faith and skepticism. They raise questions of equality and liberty, majority rule and minority rights, individual convictions and communal tradition.

The Religious Liberty provisions must be understood both in terms of the Framers' intentions and history's sometimes surprising results. Interpreting and applying them today requires not only historical research but moral and political reflection.

The intention of the Framers is therefore a necessary but insufficient criterion for interpreting and applying the Constitution. But applied by itself, without any consideration of immutable principles of justice, the intention can easily be wielded as a weapon for governmental or sectarian causes, some quoting Jefferson and brandishing No establishment and others citing Madison and brandishing Free exercise. Rather, we must take the purpose and text of the Constitution seriously, sustain the principles behind the words and add an appreciation of the many-sided genius of the First Amendment and its complex development over time.

The Consensus Must Be Dynamic

Reconstitution requires a shared understanding of the relationship between the Constitution and the society it is to serve. The Framers understood that the Constitution is more than parchment and ink. The principles embodied in the document must be affirmed in practice by a free people since these principles reflect everything that constitutes the essential forms and substance of their society—the institutions, customs and ideals as well as the laws. Civic vitality and the effectiveness of law can be undermined when they overlook this broader cultural context of the Constitution.

Notable in this connection is the striking absence today of any national consensus about religious liberty as a positive good. Yet religious liberty is indisputably what the Framers intended and what the First Amendment has preserved. Far from being a matter of exemption, exception or even toleration, religious liberty is an inalienable right. Far from being a sub-category of free speech or a constitutional redundancy, religious liberty is distinct and foundational. Far from being simply an individual right, religious liberty is a positive social good. Far from denigrating religion as a social or political "problem," the separation of Church and State is both the saving of religion from the temptation of political power and an achievement inspired in large part by religion itself. Far from weakening religion, disestablishment has, as an historical fact, enabled it to flourish.

In light of the First Amendment, the government should stand in relation to the churches, synagogues and other communities of faith as the guarantor of freedom. In light of the First Amendment, the churches, synagogues and other communities of faith stand in relation to the government as generators of faith, and therefore contribute to the spiritual and moral foundations of democracy. Thus, the government acts as a safeguard, but not the source, of freedom for faiths, whereas the churches and synagogues act as a source, but not the safeguard, of faiths for freedom.

The Religious Liberty provisions work for each other and for the federal idea as a whole. Neither established nor excluded, neither preferred nor proscribed, each faith (whether transcendent or naturalistic) is brought into a relationship with the government so that each is separated from the state in terms of its institutions, but democratically related to the state in terms of individuals and its ideas.

The result is neither a naked public square where all religion is excluded, nor a sacred public square with any religion established or semi-established. The result, rather, is a civil public square in which citizens of all religious faiths, or none, engage one another in the continuing democratic discourse.

The Compact Must Be Mutual

Reconstitution of a free republican people requires the recognition that religious liberty is a universal right joined to a universal duty to respect that right.

In the turns and twists of history, victims of religious discrimination have often later become perpetrators. In the famous image of Roger Williams, those at the helm of the Ship of State forget they were once under the hatches. They have, he said, "One weight for themselves when they are under the hatches, and another for others when they come to the helm." They show themselves, said James Madison, "as ready to set up an establishment which is to take them in as they were to pull down that which shut them out." Thus, benignly or otherwise, Protestants have treated Catholics as they were once treated, and secularists have done likewise with both.

Such inconsistencies are the natural seedbed for the growth of a de facto establishment. Against such inconsistencies we affirm that a right for one is a right for another and a responsibility for all. A right for a Protestant is a right for an Orthodox is a right for a Catholic is a right for a Jew is a right for a Humanist is a right for a Mormon is a right for a Muslim is a right for a Buddhist—and for the followers of any other faith within the wide bounds of the republic.

That rights are universal and responsibilities mutual is both the premise and the promise of democratic pluralism. The First Amendment, in this sense, is the epitome of public justice and serves as the Golden Rule for civic life. Rights are best guarded and responsibilities best exercised when each person and group guards for all others those rights they wish guarded for themselves. Whereas the wearer of the English crown is officially the Defender of the Faith, all who uphold the American Constitution are defenders of the rights of all faiths.

From this axiom, that rights are universal and responsibilities mutual, derive guidelines for conducting public debates involving religion in a manner that is democratic and civil. These guidelines are not, and must not be, mandated by law. But they are, we believe, necessary to reconstitute and revitalize the American understanding of the role of religion in a free society.

First, those who claim the right to dissent should assume the responsibility to debate: Commitment to democratic pluralism assumes the coexistence within one political community of groups whose ultimate faith commitments may be incompatible, yet whose common commitment to social unity and diversity does justice to both the requirements of individual conscience and the wider community. A general consent to the obligations of citizenship is therefore inherent in the American experiment, both as a founding principle ("We the people") and as a matter of daily practice.

There must always be room for those who do not wish to participate in the public ordering of our common life, who desire to pursue their own religious witness separately as conscience dictates. But at the same time, for those who do wish to participate, it should be understood that those claiming the right to dissent should assume the responsibility to debate. As this responsibility is exercised, the characteristic American formula of individual liberty complemented by respect for the opinions of others permits differences to be asserted, yet a broad, active community of understanding to be sustained.

Second, those who claim the right to criticize should assume the responsibility to comprehend: One of the ironies of democratic life is that freedom of conscience is jeopardized by false tolerance as well as by outright intolerance. Genuine tolerance considers contrary views fairly and judges them on merit. Debased tolerance so refrains from making any judgment that it refuses to listen at all. Genuine tolerance honestly weighs honest differences and promotes both impartiality and pluralism. Debased tolerance results in indifference to the differences that vitalize a pluralistic democracy.

Central to the difference between genuine and debased tolerance is the recognition that peace and truth must be held in tension. Pluralism must not be confused with, and is in fact endangered by, philosophical and ethical indifference. Commitment to strong, clear philosophical and ethical ideas need not imply either intolerance or opposition to democratic pluralism. On the contrary, democratic pluralism requires an agreement to be locked in public argument over disagreements of consequence within the bonds of civility.

The right to argue for any public policy is a fundamental right for every citizen; respecting that right is a fundamental responsibility for all other citizens. When any view is expressed, all must uphold as constitutionally protected its advocate's right to express it. But others are free to challenge that view as politically pernicious, philosophically false, ethically evil, theologically idolatrous, or simply absurd, as the case may be seen to be.

Unless this tension between peace and truth is respected, civility cannot be sustained. In that event, tolerance degenerates into either apathetic relativism or a dogmatism as uncritical of itself as it is uncomprehending of others. The result is a general corruption of principled public debate.

Third, those who claim the right to influence should accept the responsibility not to inflame: Too often in recent disputes over religion and public affairs, some have insisted that any evidence of religious influence on public policy represents an establishment of religion and is therefore precluded as an improper "imposition." Such exclusion of religion from public life is historically unwarranted, philosophically inconsistent and profoundly undemocratic. The Framers' intention is indisputably ignored when public policy debates can appeal to the theses of Adam Smith and Karl Marx, or Charles Darwin and Sigmund Freud but not to the Western religious tradition in general and the Hebrew and Christian Scriptures in particular. Many of the most dynamic social movements in American history, including that of civil rights, were legitimately inspired and shaped by religious motivation.

Freedom of conscience and the right to influence public policy on the basis of religiously informed ideas are inseverably linked. In short, a key to democratic renewal is the fullest possible participation in the most open possible debate.

Religious liberty and democratic civility are also threatened, however, from another quarter. Overreacting to an improper veto on religion in public life, many have used religious language and images not for the legitimate influencing of policies but to inflame politics. Politics is indeed an extension of ethics and therefore engages religious principles; but some err by refusing to recognize that there is a distinction, though not a separation, between religion and politics. As a result, they bring to politics a misplaced absoluteness that idolizes politics, "Satanizes" their enemies and politicizes their own faith.

Even the most morally informed policy positions involve prudential judgments as well as pure principle. Therefore, to make an absolute equation of principles and policies inflates politics and does violence to reason, civil life and faith itself. Politics has recently been inflamed by a number of confusions: the confusion of personal religious affiliation with qualification or disqualification for public office; the confusion of claims to divine guidance with claims to divine endorsement; and the confusion of government neutrality among faiths with government indifference or hostility to religion.

Fourth, those who claim the right to participate should accept the responsibility to persuade: Central to the American experience is the power of political persuasion. Growing partly from principle and partly from the pressures of democratic pluralism, commitment to persuasion is the corollary of the belief that conscience is inviolable, coercion of conscience is evil, and the public interest is best served by consent hard won from vigorous debate.

Those who believe themselves privy to the will of history brook no argument and need never tarry for consent. But to those who subscribe to the idea of government by the consent of the governed, compelled beliefs are a violation of first principles. The natural logic of the Religious Liberty provisions is to foster a political culture of persuasion which admits the challenge of opinions from all sources.

Arguments for public policy should be more than private convictions shouted out loud. For persuasion to be principled, private convictions should be translated into publicly accessible claims. Such public claims should be made publicly accessible for two reasons: first, because they must engage those who do not share the same private convictions, and second, because they should be directed toward the common good.

Renewal of First Principles

We who live in the third century of the American republic can learn well from the past as we look to the future. Our Founders were both idealists and realists. Their confidence in human abilities was tempered by their skepticism about human nature. Aware of what was new in their times, they also knew the need for renewal in times after theirs. "No free government, or the blessings of liberty," wrote George Mason in 1776, "can be preserved to any people, but by a firm adherence to justice, moderation, temperance, frugality, and virtue, and by frequent recurrence to fundamental principles."

True to the ideals and realism of that vision, we who sign this Charter, people of many and various beliefs, pledge ourselves to the enduring precepts of the First Amendment as the cornerstone of the American experiment in liberty under law.

We address ourselves to our fellow citizens, daring to hope that the strongest desire of the greatest number is for the common good. We are firmly persuaded that the principles asserted here require a fresh consideration, and that the renewal of religious liberty is crucial to sustain a free people that would remain free. We therefore commit ourselves to speak, write and act according to this vision and these principles. We urge our fellow citizens to do the same.

To agree on such guiding principles and to achieve such a compact will not be easy. Whereas a law is a command directed to us, a compact is a promise that must proceed freely from us. To achieve it demands a measure of the vision, sacrifice and perseverance shown by our Founders. Their task was to defy the past, seeing and securing religious liberty against the terrible precedents of history. Ours is to challenge the future, sustaining vigilance and broadening protections against every new menace, including that of our own complacency. Knowing the unquenchable desire for freedom, they lit a beacon. It is for us who know its blessings to keep it burning brightly.

Acknowledgments

A book like this one, which is the product of many years of thinking in many different situations, owes a debt of gratitude to more people than I could mention. But my ingratitude would be monstrous if I did not thank the following:

Doug and Ann Holladay, whose warm invitation to come to the United States for six months has led to a stay of more than twenty years, throughout which their friendship has been rich and central.

James H. Billington, formerly of the Woodrow Wilson Center for International Studies, and Bruce K. McLaury, formerly of The Brookings Institution, whose hospitality toward me as a visiting fellow at their respective institutions gave me the opportunity to study and discuss what had long been a private passion.

Bob Kramer, Al MacDonald, William J. Flynn, John Seel, and Tom McWhertor, whose collegiality and hard work made the bicentennial project of the Williamsburg Charter into an exciting, if arduous, adventure.

Ed Gaffney, Charles Haynes, Alan Mittleman, Richard John Neuhaus, Buzz Thomas, and George Weigel, whom in the course of fighting for religious liberty I discovered to be friends and fellow advocates of the first liberty.

Jamin Warren, for his careful research and painstaking checking of references.

Bob Cochran, Mike Cromartie, Charles Haynes, Dick Ohman, David Wells, and Peggy Wehmeyer Woods, friends who read this manuscript in its entirety and made many invaluable suggestions. What remains is completely my responsibility; while their contributions, though decisive, are invisible and known only to heaven and them.

Mickey Maudlin, Roger Freet, Jan Weed, Kris Ashley, Laurie Dunne, Helena Brantley, and all the editorial team at HarperOne, with whom it is a pleasure to work and is an honor to publish.

Notes

Chapter One: A World Safe for Diversity

1. See Jonathan Glover, *Humanity: A Moral History of the Twentieth Century* (London: Jonathan Cape, 1999); and Os Guinness, *Unspeakable: Facing Up to the Challenge of Evil* (San Francisco: HarperSanFrancisco, 2005).

2. Quoted in Michael Burleigh, *Sacred Causes: The Clash of Religion and Politics, from the Great War to the War on Terror* (New York: HarperCollins, 2007), 135.

3. Ambrose Bierce, *The Devil's Dictionary* (New York: Dover Publications, 1993).

4. See Edward T. Shils, *The Virtue of Civility: Selected Essays on Liberalism, Tradition, and Civil Society* (Indianapolis: Liberty Fund, 1997), 320–355.

5. Geoffrey Hindley, *A Brief History of the Crusades* (London: Constable & Robinson, 2004), 256.

6. Hindley, *Brief History,* 260.

7. President John F. Kennedy, "Spring Commencement Address," American University, June 10, 1963.

8. Peter L. Berger, ed., *The Desecularization of the World: Resurgent Religion and World Politics* (Grand Rapids, MI: William B. Eerdmans, 1999), 2.

9. Pericles, "The Funeral Oration," in *History of the Peloponnesian War,* trans. Rex Warner (London: Penguin Classics, 1954), 147.

10. Richard Sennett, *The Fall of Public Man* (New York: Alfred A. Knopf, 1992); Wendell Berry, *Sex, Economy, Freedom and Community* (New York: Pantheon Books, 1992), 133.

11. See James Davison Hunter and Alan Wolfe, *Is There a Culture War? A Dialogue on Values and American Public Life* (Washington, DC: Brookings Institution Press, 2006).

12. Gertrude Himmelfarb, *One Nation, Two Cultures* (New York: Alfred A. Knopf, 1999), 20.

13. *The View,* September 5, 2006.

14. James Madison, "Memorial and Remonstrance," *The Papers of James Madison*, vol. 2, ed. William T. Hutchison (Chicago: Univ. of Chicago Press, 1962).

Chapter Two: The True Remedy

1. André Malraux, quoted in Richard John Neuhaus, *The Best of "The Public Square"* (Grand Rapids, MI: Eerdmans, 2001), 11.

2. Professor Peter L. Berger, Boston University, in public remarks.

3. Berger, *Desecularization of the World*, 2.

4. William Lee Miller, *First Liberty: Religion and the American Republic*, 308.

5. Address of Osama bin Laden, "This War Is Fundamentally Religious," November 7, 2001, http://www.washingtonpost.com/.

6. See George Weigel, *The Cube and the Cathedral: Europe, America, and Politics Without God* (New York: Basic Books, 2003).

7. Thomas Jefferson to Thomas Law, June 13, 1814, quoted in James H. Hutson, *The Founders on Religion* (Princeton: Princeton Univ. Press, 2005), 22.

8. See Grace Davie, *Europe: The Exceptional Case* (London: Darton, Longman and Todd, 2002).

9. Davie, *Europe*, 10.

10. Quoted in Richard Dawkins, *The God Delusion* (Boston: Houghton Mifflin Company, 2006), 14.

11. Peter Berger, Boston University, in public remarks.

12. Peter Berger, Boston University, in public remarks.

13. Quoted in Michael Burleigh, *Earthly Powers* (London: Harper-Collins, 2005), 81.

14. Davie, *Europe*, 19.

15. Alexis de Tocqueville, *Democracy in America*, trans. Gerald E. Bevan (London: Penguin Books, 2003), 345.

16. Tocqueville, *Democracy in America*, 342.

17. Quoted in Richard Labunski, *James Madison and the Struggle for the Bill of Rights* (New York: Oxford Univ. Press, 2006), 227.

18. James Madison to William Bradford, 1772, quoted in Labunski, *James Madison*, 163.

19. Thomas Jefferson, "The Virginia Statute on Religious Liberty," in *Statutes at Large of Virginia*, ed. W. W. Henning (1823), 12:84.

20. George Washington, quoted in Stanley Weintraub, *General Washington's Christmas Farewell* (New York: Simon & Schuster, 2003), 67.

21. Thomas Jefferson, quoted in Patricia Bonomi, *Under the Cope of Heaven: Religion, Society, and Politics in Colonial America* (New York, Oxford Univ. Press, 1986), 210.

22. George Washington, quoted in Abiel Holmes, *The Annals of America from the Discovery by Columbus in the Year 1492 to the Year 1826* (Cambridge: Hillard and Brown, 1986), 210.

23. Madison, "Memorial and Remonstrance."

24. Robert Putnam, *Bowling Alone: The Collapse and Revival of American Community* (New York: Simon and Schuster, 2000), 66.

25. Katherine Harris, "Rep. Harris Condemns Separation of Church, State," *Orlando Sentinel* (August 26, 2006), A09.

26. Tocqueville, *Democracy in America,* 341.

27. "Letter of Pope Gelasius to Emperor Anastasius," in *Readings in European History,* trans. J. H. Robinson (Boston: Ginn, 1905), 72–73.

28. David Kuo, *Tempting Faith: An Inside Story of Political Seduction* (New York: Free Press, 2006), 209.

29. Quoted in Burleigh, *Earthly Powers,* 139.

30. Tocqueville, *Democracy in America,* vol. 2, chap. 5.

31. Quoted in Barbara M. Cross, ed., *The Autobiography of Lyman Beecher* (Cambridge, MA: Harvard Univ. Press, 1961), 1:251.

32. Lyman Beecher "A Plea for the West," in Cross, *Autobiography of Lyman Beecher,* 1:253.

Chapter Three: The Broken Settlement

1. Colin Joyce, "Why Japanese Girls Want Christmas Romance," *Daily Telegraph,* December 22, 2006.

2. Voltaire, *Letters Concerning the English Nation* (London: J and R Tonson, 1778), 38.

3. *The Williamsburg Charter Survey on Religion and Public Life* (Washington, DC: Williamsburg Charter Foundation, 1988).

4. Harold L. Hodgkinson, *California: The State and Its Educational Sysem* (Washington, DC: Institute for Educational Leadership, 1986).

5. Harold J. Berman, "The Challenge of the Modern State," in *Articles of Faith, Articles of Peace,* ed. James Davison Hunter and Os Guinness (Washington, DC: Brookings Institution Press, 1990), 48.

6. Berman, "The Challenge of the Modern State," 43.

7. James Davison Hunter, "Religious Freedom and the Challenge of Modern Pluralism," in *Articles of Faith, Articles of Peace,* ed. James Davison Hunter, Os Guinness (Washington, DC: Brookings Institution Press, 1990), 54f.

8. Letters to Moses Robinson, 1801.

9. Hutson, *Founders on Religion*, 96.

10. Quoted in Bernard Bailyn, *To Begin the World Anew* (New York: Alfred A. Knopf, 2003), 49.

11. Bailyn, *To Begin the World Anew*, 93.

12. Bailyn, *To Begin the World Anew*, 84.

13. Bailyn, *To Begin the World Anew*, 91.

14. Bailyn, *To Begin the World Anew*, 93.

15. Hutson, *Founders on Religion*, 97.

16. *Everson v. Board of Education of Ewing Township*, 330 U.S. 1 (1947).

Chapter Four: Say No to the Sacred Public Square

1. See David Aikman, *Jesus in Beijing* (Washington, DC: Regnery Press, 2003).

2. See Julian P. Boyd, "On the Need for 'Frequent Recurrence to Fundamental Principles,'" *Virginia Law Review* 62, no. 5 (June 1976), 859–871; Thomas Jefferson to William S. Smith, November, 13, 1787, in *The Political Writings of Thomas Jefferson*, ed. Merrill D. Petersen (Chapel Hill: Univ. of North Carolina Press, 1993).

3. Fareed Zakaria, *The Future of Freedom: Illiberal Democracy at Home and Abroad* (New York: W.W. Norton & Company, 2004), 26.

4. James Davison Hunter, "The Discourse of Negation and the Ironies of Common Culture," *Hedgehog Review*, Fall 2004, 28.

5. Quoted in Conor Cruise O'Brien, *Edmund Burke* (Dublin: New Island Books, 1997), 14.

6. Kevin Phillips, *American Theocracy: The Peril and Politics of Radical Religion, Oil, and Borrowed Money in the 21st Century* (New York: Viking Books, 2006), 208.

7. Luke 6:27, 28.

8. Quoted in Burleigh, *Sacred Causes*, 12.

9. Wendell Berry, *Citizenship Papers* (Washington, DC: Shoemaker & Hoard, 2003), 14.

10. "War on Christians Is Alleged," *Washington Post*, March 29, 2006, A 12.

11. Theologian Paul Althaus in lectures in 1932, quoted in Burleigh, *Sacred Causes*, 108.

12. Quoted in Burleigh, *Sacred Causes*, 108.

13. Quoted in Hermann Dorries, *Constantine the Great*, trans. Roland H. Bainton (New York: Harper & Row, 1972), 152.

14. Quoted in Burleigh, *Sacred Causes*, 102.
15. Tocqueville, *Democracy in America*, 1:342.
16. Hunter and Wolfe, *Is There a Culture War*, 95.
17. Richard John Neuhaus, in numerous public remarks.

Chapter Five: Say No to the Naked Public Square

1. Bertrand Russell, "A Free Man's Worship," in *Why I Am Not a Christian* (New York: Simon & Schuster, 1957), 107.
2. See, for instance, Alister McGrath, *Dawkins' God: Genes, Memes, and the Meaning of Life* (Oxford: Blackwell, 2006), which devastates Dawkins, who refers to the book as fair but carries on with his original arguments as if they had never been challenged.
3. Dawkins, *God Delusion*, 5.
4. Sam Harris, *The End of Faith: Religion, Terror, and the Future of Reason* (New York: W. W. Norton, 2005), 227.
5. Sam Harris, *Letter to a Christian Nation* (New York: Alfred A. Knopf, 2006), 91.
6. Quoted in Gary Wolfe, "The Church of the Non-Believers," *Wired*, November 2006, 190.
7. Harris, *End of Faith*, 23, 46.
8. Richard John Neuhaus, *The Naked Public Square: Religion and Democracy in America* (Grand Rapids, MI: William B. Eerdmans, 1984).
9. See Noah Feldman, *Divided by God: America's Church-State Problem and What We Should Do About It* (New York: Farrar, Straus, and Giroux, 2005).
10. Rodney Stark, *One True God: Historical Consequences of Monotheism* (Princeton, NJ: Princeton Univ. Press, 2001), 251.
11. Thomas Paine, *The Age of Reason: Being an Investigation of True and Fabulous Theology* in *The Complete Writings of Thomas Paine*, ed. Philip S. Foner (New York: Citadel Press, 1945), 1:460
12. John Gray, *Heresies* (London: Granta Books, 2004), 41.
13. Dawkins, *God Delusion*, 303.
14. John Gray, *Two Faces of Liberalism* (New York: New Press, 2000), 8.
15. Quoted in Harvey J. Kaye, *Thomas Paine and the Promise of America* (New York: Hill and Wang, 2005), 74.
16. Quoted in Jonathan Sacks, "Judaism and Politics," in Berger, *Desecularization of the World*, 52.
17. Burleigh, *Sacred Causes*, xvi.

18. Daniel Driesbach, "Origins and Dangers of 'The Wall of Separation' Between Church and State," *Imprimis,* October 2006, 5.

19. Abraham Lincoln, "Address to Lyceum" in *Lincoln: Selected Speeches and Writings* (New York: Vintage Books, Random House, 1992), 14.

20. John Milton, *The Terror of Kings and Magistrates*, ed. William Talbot Allison (first published 1649; New York: Henry Holt, 1911).

21. Roger Williams, *The Bloudy Tenent of Persecutions, for the Cause of Conscience*, vol. 3 (first published 1644; Providence, RI: Publications of the Navaganseth Club, 1867).

22. Pope Benedict XVI [Joseph Ratzinger], *Christianity and the Crisis of Cultures*, trans. Brian McNeil (San Francisco: Ignatius Press, 2006), 36.

Chapter Six: A Cosmopolitan and Civil Public Square

1. Gouverneur Morris to William Carmichael, July 10, 1789, in *The Life and Writings of Gouverneur Morris*, ed. Jared Sparks (Boston: Gray and Bowen, 1832), 2:75.

2. Feldman, *Divided by God,* 237.

3. Quoted in Kevin Seamus Hasson, *The Right to Be Wrong* (San Francisco: Encounter Books, 2005), 139.

4. Alexander Hamilton, *The Federalist Papers*, no 1, in *The Federalist Papers*, ed. Clinton Rossite (New York: Signet Classics, 2003).

5. Daniel J. Elazar, *Covenant and Polity in Biblical Israel* (New Brunswick, NJ: Transaction Publishers, 1998), 401.

6. Zygmunt Bauman, *In Search of Politics* (Stanford, CA: Stanford Univ. Press, 1999), 155.

7. Miller, *First Liberty,* 259.

8. David Hackett Fischer, *Freedom and Liberty* (New York: Oxford Univ. Press, 2005), 233.

9. Ulrich Beck, *Power in the Global Age: A New Global Political Economy* (London: Polity Press, 2005), xvi.

10. See John Courtney Murray, *We Hold These Truths* (New York: Sheed and Ward 1960).

11. John Gray, *Enlightenment's Wake: Politics and Culture at the Close of the Modern Age* (London: Routledge, 1995), 67.

12. Murray, *We Hold These Truths*, 86.

13. Thomas Jefferson to Jacob De La Motta, September 1, 1820. Papers of Thomas Jefferson, Library of Congress, Manuscript Division.

14. George Weigel, "Achieving Disagreement," *This World* (Winter 1989), 87.

15. Dawkins, *God Delusion*, 306.

16. Quoted in Wolfe, "Church of the Non-Believers," 186.

17. Quoted in Wolfe, "Church of the Non-Believers," 184.

18. Quoted in Miller, *First Liberty*, 202.

19. Quoted in Ramsay MacMullen, *Christianity and Paganism in the Fourth to Eighth Centuries* (New Haven, CT: Yale Univ. Press, 1997), 130.

20. Michel de Montaigne, *On Friendship*, trans. M. A. Screech (London: Penguin Books, 1991), 34.

21. John Milton, *Areopagitica: A Speech for the Liberty of Unlicensed Printing*, vol. 14 (first published 1644; Cambridge: The Harvard Classics, 1909).

22. Quoted in Bernard Semmel, *The Methodist Revolution* (New York: Basic Books, 1973), 88.

23. William Hague, *William Pitt the Younger* (London: HarperCollins, 2004), 331.

24. Friedrich Nietzsche, *Ecce Homo*, trans. W. Kaufman (New York: Vintage, 1967), 326-27.

Chapter Seven: Starting with Ourselves

1. For practical examples, see Charles C. Haynes, Sam Chaltain, and Susan M. Glissom, eds., *First Freedoms: A Documentary History of First Amendment Rights in America* (New York: Oxford Univ. Press, 2006), 210–12.

2. Henrik Ibsen, *An Enemy of the People* (London: Heinemann, 1967), act 5.

Index